"Benjamin Watson has kn[...]
The New Dad's Playbook has commonsense information,
augmented by biblical principles, specifically directed at men
who are starting a family. If you're a man preparing for your
first child, you must read this book. If you already have children, you'll want to read it as you continue to grow your
family."

Tony Dungy, bestselling author of
Quiet Strength and *Uncommon*

"Benjamin Watson has written exactly what we need. We
need honest, understanding, and inviting words on fatherhood. I'm certain this book will be a guide to new fathers
for years to come."

Drew Brees, NFL quarterback, New Orleans Saints

"Benjamin dives into each aspect of fatherhood that will help
husbands connect with the hearts of their wives and prepare
for one of the most important callings a man can have. Every
new dad and dad-to-be needs this resource!"

Lysa TerKeurst, *New York Times* bestselling author
and president of Proverbs 31 Ministries

"As a father of six and a grandfather of two, I've read plenty
of 'new dad' books over the years, with instructions on diaper
changing and how to hold your baby. Well, if you want to
take it to the next level, Benjamin Watson's *The New Dad's
Playbook* is a must read. This is not just a book about being
the best dad you can be. It is also about being the very best
husband you can be during what is a life-changing, rock-your-
world nine months. Benjamin's wealth of advice, counseling,

and encouragement comes from experience, and you'll be so grateful that he chose to share it. This book is like Ben—a winner!"

Ernie Johnson Jr., TNT sportscaster
and author of *Unscripted*

"If you want to be a helpful husband to your wife when she needs you most, and if you want to be a great father to your baby, then *The New Dad's Playbook* is for you! I am amazed at how thorough and well researched this book is and I was blown away at how often I acknowledged, "Yup . . . I made that mistake too!" Like me, you will want to thank Benjamin from the bottom of your heart for genuinely helping you become an overnight better husband and father after reading *The New Dad's Playbook*."

Drew Rosenhaus, NFL agent

"There aren't many books out there that quite lay out the groundwork like this one. This book will empower new dads to know their role on the team and new moms to be fully supported and cared for. That's a win!"

Candace Cameron Bure, actress, author,
and cohost of *The View*

THE
NEW DAD'S
PLAYBOOK

THE
NEW DAD'S
PLAYBOOK

GEARING UP FOR THE
BIGGEST GAME OF YOUR LIFE

BENJAMIN
WATSON

BakerBooks
a division of Baker Publishing Group
Grand Rapids, Michigan

© 2017 by Benjamin Watson

Published by Baker Books
a division of Baker Publishing Group
P.O. Box 6287, Grand Rapids, MI 49516-6287
www.bakerbooks.com

Printed in the United States of America

Library of Congress Cataloging-in-Publication Data
Names: Watson, Benjamin, 1980 December 18– author.
Title: The new dad's playbook : gearing up for the biggest game of your life / Benjamin Watson.
Description: Grand Rapids : Baker Books, 2017. | Includes bibliographical references.
Identifiers: LCCN 2016057223 | ISBN 9780801018978 (pbk.)
Subjects: LCSH: Fatherhood—Religious aspects—Christianity. | Pregnancy— Religious aspects—Christianity.
Classification: LCC BV4529.17 .W37 2017 | DDC 248.8/421—dc23
LC record available at https://lccn.loc.gov/2016057223

17 18 19 20 21 22 23   10 9 8 7 6 5 4

green press INITIATIVE

To my beautiful wife,
whose selfless devotion to our family
inspires me to be a more loving husband,
a more caring father,
and a more godly man.

Contents

Contents

Foreword

Several years ago I was chatting with Benjamin on the phone and he mentioned that he was considering writing a manual for fathers in order to help them through the pregnancy and birthing process. I was thrilled. "Of course you should write this book," I remember telling him. "The world needs to hear from great men and fathers!" Little did I know then what I know now—that Benjamin was not going to write a simple manual of how-tos for fathers, but rather he was going to write a masterpiece. And that is exactly what this book is: a masterpiece that combines clear guidance for fathers on what they need to do, how they need to think, and why they should lean on God during one of the most challenging and precious times in their lives. It is not a simple guidebook on fathering. Benjamin gives the reader a peek into how men experience a process that, for far too long, has been written about only to help mothers. I am so proud that he has cracked the mold and been courageous enough to speak on behalf of the overlooked parents—dads.

As a pediatrician of thirty years, I have listened to literally thousands of fathers. I have heard your stories about how you feel excluded from bonding with your babies, your fear over what pregnancy and child-rearing may do to your relationships with your wives, and also your doubts about whether you have what it takes to be great dads. I know firsthand how critical you are in your children's lives because I have seen the pain your wives and children feel when you leave. And I have been blessed to watch many more of you fathers hang in there through the rough times with your wives and kids. I am thrilled to know that after you read this book, you will have more encouragement, more knowledge, and a clearer sense of your deep value to your children and to their mothers. *We need you good men.*

Benjamin will teach you many things about pregnancy and birthing that you never knew. I learned many things from reading this book, and in fact, I wish that my own physician husband had this book when I was pregnant! Benjamin teaches men in a gentle but firm way how they can help their wives. He shows us women how men think and what you feel while we are pregnant. After reading this, I felt badly for all of the men who have gone through their wives' pregnancies and not had necessary help. The truth is, encouraging, teaching, and supporting fathers on all levels is long overdue in America. It is high time that we women pay attention to the fathers of our children. In that vein, I encourage every pregnant woman to read this book too. But I will issue a warning: you will feel jealous of Benjamin's wife, Kirsten, for a while, because she hit the jackpot when it comes to husbands! Benjamin describes being able to read her moods and figure out what type of help made her feel most loved—gifts, time, or rest. And you will read that he even sat in a football locker room and ordered her maternity clothes! See what I mean? I honestly have never known another man who has done that. But those character qualities—kindness, empathy, and insight—are what make Benjamin the perfect author of this book. He lives what he teaches. He is the real deal.

There are many parenting books available, but none has been written with such heart as this one. In fact, even if you aren't a parent, you should read it, because you will learn some very important lessons on relationships, love, and how to live a good life. I am especially proud that a man such as Benjamin—an NFL pro—wrote this book, because he is a hero to many men (and women). By playing an elite sport and writing such a heartfelt, information-packed book, he redefines masculinity. He shows us that men can be strong and tough but also kind and compassionate enough to parent really well.

My hope for this book is that the words Benjamin writes and the lives that he changes through it will begin a new revolution for men. Fathers need to regain their rightful place in the family and be encouraged to bond with their children. Studies show that when a baby, child, or teenager has a good father, that child will soar. Specifically, when a child feels connected to his or her dad, he or she is less likely to get into trouble at school, suffer from depression and anxiety, or get involved with sex, drugs, and alcohol, and is more likely to graduate from high school and go on to college. I have written about these phenomena in my parenting books. As a staunch child advocate, I have read the literature about the impact that fathers make on their children, and it is over-whelmingly clear: dads change their kids' lives. The choice they have is this: Will they change their children's lives for the better or for the worse?

Reading this book will help any father anywhere be a better parent. Period. And it will help fathers enjoy parenting more. As a pediatrician, I will say that all fathers or fathers-to-be need to read it. And they need their wives to read it so that mothers can finally see how fathers feel. We women need to know what to do to help you. And—this is hard for many mothers to swallow—we mothers need to give up some parenting territory and let you dads in. You need to be rocking and feeding babies because those babies need to bond with fathers too. We need to engage you in the pregnancy process and quit being so controlling about parenting. Breast-feeding is wonderful, but many fathers feel excluded from bonding because they can't feed their babies. So we need to encourage fathers to put breast milk in a bottle and feed their children. This is not only fair but is important to the health of the father-child relationship.

If you are a mother or father, I am so happy that you picked up this book. Don't stop reading. Turn the pages and let the great advice contained there soak in. Learning about pregnancy and birth from a whole new perspective will open your eyes. And then, when you have finished, give a copy to the newest expectant father that you know. He will thank you, his wife will thank you, but most importantly, you will do a great service to the wonderful children that he raises.

Meg Meeker, MD

Introduction

You may be familiar with Benjamin Watson, the NFL football player and Super Bowl champion, but you may not know that in addition to giving his best on the gridiron, he's also a dedicated husband and daddy. Benjamin and I have been married since 2005, and together we have been blessed with five children ages seven, six, four, three, and nine months. Our house is busy, noisy (except for when the kids are eating or sleeping), and full of laughter, bike riding, mud-pie making, and tons of pretend play. Although I'm the primary parent at home during the day, when Benjamin is home, our family just "clicks" and we run like a well-oiled machine. I know the hours Benjamin has given during his twelve years in the NFL to be the best football player he can be. Whether spending extra time at the gym, experimenting with different workouts that will make him faster and stronger, or playing with an injury, he gives 100 percent of himself on the field. Benjamin is also committed to us. He loves us, and he pours his heart even more into being a better husband and daddy than a better football player. It may surprise you to learn that Benjamin is a big part of keeping our family strong. He is as committed to raising our children as he is to winning championships.

You may be wondering, "What makes Benjamin qualified to write a parenting book?" I can assure you that the pages you are about to read are honest and true. Benjamin believes that it is his duty as a father to be a positive role model for our kids. He practices what he preaches, and after our five pregnancies and deliveries, he's had the opportunity to get it right! He did not do everything perfectly, but he was willing to learn and try doing things differently. He changes diapers, cooks, cleans, gives baths, does "daddy-daughter date nights," reads books, and becomes the kids' real-life jungle gym. He also asks for forgiveness from, disciplines, and prays with all of them. Much of what we do is modeled after our amazing parents, but we've learned a lot on our own family journey, and we hope that sharing our experiences will encourage, empower, and excite you as you start your own.

Benjamin assisted with all five of our deliveries. Notice that I said "assisted" and not "attended." There is a *big* difference. All five were different, and what I needed with each one changed. It's important for fathers to have an understanding of what's going on with their wives during the nine months of pregnancy, the delivery, and postpartum. Let me just say that it behooves a husband to be able to decipher his wife's mood swings and bodily changes. If you know why it's happening in the first place, it may prevent you from saying, "Wow! You're getting huge!" (which, even if you don't read past this page, *please don't ever say*) and instead give her a simple hug or gentle caress of the abdomen to make her feel comforted and loved. Trust me, men, let Benjamin's mistakes help you get things right the first time!

Benjamin has included checklists throughout the book to help you stay organized and on top of your game. He has a strong parental instinct and drive, similar to what makes him such an excellent athlete. His experiences can be educational for you. As you'll see in the following pages, a great fatherly drive doesn't ensure perfection every day. Your child needs *both* imperfect parents. Your presence and your commitment to your family are more important than checking off all the "best father ever" milestones. Love, support, and guidance through meaningful engagement are what your growing family needs, and you'll discover some of the ways to do that here.

So whether you picked this book up to read on your own or it was given to you with a slight "threat" to finish it before the baby comes (*wink, wink*), be encouraged. You have a cheat sheet that is going to help you not be Benjamin, but be the best father *you* can be, and always be thinking about how you can be better. Regardless of the personal relationship you have with your own father, you have to aim to be better. There are no excuses. Your wife needs you. Your baby needs you. And you can do it.

Benjamin and I are believers in Jesus Christ. I believe that this spiritual strength gives us the ability to be real role models for our children. We see our children as secret weapons for making the world a better place. It's our responsibility to raise them to love Jesus and love others. If we do this, perhaps their love and light will guide others to the kingdom. I am often reminded of the words in Psalm 127:3–5:

> Children are a heritage from the LORD,
> offspring a reward from him.
> Like arrows in the hands of a warrior
> are children born in one's youth.

Blessed is the man
whose quiver is full of them.
They will not be put to shame
when they contend with their opponents in court.

Children are God's blessing, and we do not take that responsibility lightly. We have been entrusted with the important work of molding our children in the image of the Lord.

Women may bring babies into the world, but fathers are critical in raising healthy, happy children. Don't let society tell you that you are only worth as much as you bank. I couldn't imagine doing this by myself, and our children's relationship with Benjamin is one that I could never replace or duplicate. Your physical and emotional presence is crucial, and your children know it even from the womb. Our youngest child would do somersaults in utero whenever Benjamin came into a room and started talking—she could feel his presence, and their bond remains strong. All of our children are better for having a strong, loving father in their lives. And yours will be too.

Kirsten Watson

PART 1

TRAINING CAMP

CHAPTER ONE

Where's the Fatherhood Playbook?

Most men dream of becoming fathers one day. If you are one of those men, or if you have recently learned that you are about to join the ranks, this book will show you how to have a positive, lifelong influence on your growing family, starting as soon as you hear the happy news.

I became a father to my first daughter, Grace, in 2009. She was due on Super Bowl Sunday, of all days. At that time, I was in the National Football League (NFL) playing for the New England Patriots. Since we hadn't made it to the playoffs that year, I planned to spend Super Bowl Sunday at home with my wife, Kirsten, waiting for our lives to change. Grace came a day or two early, so we watched the game in the recovery room. I was twenty-eight years old, and my wife and I had been married for three years. Grace is now seven years old, and since her arrival we have been blessed with four other children: Naomi, age five; Isaiah, four; Judah, three; and Eden, who is nine months old.

Kirsten and I thought we were prepared for parenthood—we were both fortunate to have excellent role models during our childhoods. My mother and father raised me and my five younger siblings, but being the oldest came with responsibility, which meant changing diapers and feeding my baby brothers and sisters. My wife also grew up in a tight-knit family. But there were still plenty of times after we brought Grace home that it felt like we had forgotten everything we knew about child-raising.

Currently, I am a tight end for the NFL's Baltimore Ravens, and a lot of my teammates are having their first children, so they see me as something of an expert on fatherhood. They come to me with their parenting and pregnancy questions. Many of these guys remind me of how I felt before Grace was born—they think they know what is coming, but they don't.

The Road of Discovery

Preparing for a new baby, especially a first baby, is a long road of discovery. Good luck finding the equivalent of *What to Expect When You're Expecting* for men. One minute your wife tells you that you are having a baby, the next you are running out of the house at midnight to buy her a pint of ice cream. Before you know it, you are in the delivery room squeezing her hand and waiting to hear your baby's first cry. Amid the rush of adrenaline and surging emotions, visitors come and go, and soon enough you are all told to go home. You find yourself standing at the hospital exit hazily thinking to yourself, *Wait, I know we had almost a year to prepare, but I have no idea what to do now!*

I was nervous with Grace because there seemed to be better directions for assembling a bicycle than there were for taking care of a newborn child. No matter how many of my brothers' and sisters' diapers I had changed, I still felt unprepared. I made a few errors along the way, but I learned from them and eventually developed a solid game plan for facing challenges with my other children. I hope this book will spare you some of my fumbles and provide you with a path to parenting success.

Fear of the Unknown Is Natural

Most men are scared or nervous when they hear they are going to become a father. Then, when they hold their child in their arms for the first time, they feel elation and pride and wonder how they can avoid hurting this fragile creature. What if you cause harm without even knowing you are doing something wrong? I don't care how many Super Bowl rings you wear, what your job title is, or what kind of car you drive, when your wife is pregnant for the first time, many men would rather turn the other way than ask, "How do I do this? How can I help?"

This book is for those guys: You don't have to wing it for the next nine to twelve months—in fact, you shouldn't! I hope I can provide guidance for those of you scratching your heads and wondering where you fit into this whole process.

In the conversations I have with men about to become first-time fathers, I hear it all:

- "Is my wife going to be overreacting, vomiting, and pushing me away in bed until the baby arrives?"
- "My brother-in-law said something about labor lasting twenty-four hours—how can my wife push that long?"
- "I really want a boy to toss the ball around with, but we're having a girl. I'm disappointed and don't know what to do."
- "How do you hold something so small without breaking it?"

These questions are honest and sincere. Contrary to popular belief, many men want to be a part of the pregnancy process. They want to be the best partners possible to the women who are bringing their children into the world.

The first few days after your child's birth are a blur, and if you don't prepare beforehand, you will be overwhelmed. When you are exhausted—and you will be—the smallest problem can send you into a panic. For example, if your baby needs to eat every two hours, and she's not eating well, you will spin all sorts of worst-case scenarios in your mind, when she probably just needs a good burp.

Finding the Answers

As men, we want to have all the answers, and as you read this book, I hope you will be open to the process. Life will not always run smoothly—your wife's experiences will tax her emotions as well as her body. Her moods, energy level, sex drive, and even taste buds will change with each trimester. Most guys say, "Well, yeah, we know this," but thinking you understand is no substitute for living alongside a pregnant woman for nine months. This book will provide the inside scoop on what it takes to be a pro partner and a pro dad from the moment you hear the happy news.

Men want to know we can solve anything, that we can handle all of life's demands. Even when we have successful careers and meet our soul mates, we may still experience self-doubt at times. Perhaps there is never a more poignant moment in a man's life than the day he discovers he is going to become a father. Perhaps, too, there is never a day when he experiences such a sudden flash of fear as when he wonders, *Am I ready to be a father?* This scares many men, but what they don't know is that with a little preparation, they will get through the rough patches and be rewarded with a beautiful, healthy family.

Your wife will go through the pregnancy, and along the way there will be pain, tears, and perhaps a few fights. There will be unforgettable joyous occasions, like when you first hear the baby's heartbeat, when you find out the sex of the baby, or when you feel the baby kick. Then your wife will deliver the baby, and you will all go home. Together. Soon enough the challenges of raising a baby will arise: the baby may cry all night, or stop nursing, and you will fear you are failing or causing irreversible damage. I'm going to let you in on a little secret: parenting isn't rocket science, but employing a little common sense and preparation can go a long way in keeping you and your spouse sane. (Sleep deprivation, however, is unavoidable. Get used to it.)

Children Need Fathers

Fatherhood, and parenting in general, is the most important job on earth, but the job doesn't come with instructions.

You may feel like God let you off easy by making you a man when you see your wife kneeling on the bathroom floor battling morning sickness. You may also wish you could spare your wife all the harsh elements of pregnancy, but you can't.

Do not forget this: you have a very important role in raising this child by laying a solid foundation for your growing family, by being present, and by following some of the suggestions laid out in this book. To quote my former coach Bill Belichick, "Do your job."

When my wife, Kirsten, experienced morning sickness during her first pregnancy, all I could do was sit down next to her on the bathroom floor and hold her. Years later, when I overheard somebody ask her what the sweetest thing I had ever done for her during her first pregnancy was, she answered, "When I had morning sickness, Benjamin held me."

Of course, I wanted to run interference, call the doctor, and get medicine to ease Kirsten's pain, but my presence was exactly what she needed. Your presence speaks volumes about your commitment to your family. It means you are totally invested in the pregnancy and in the health of the mother. Knowing she has your support is paramount to the well-being of everyone involved.

The woman carrying your child is experiencing hormonal changes, and when she knows you are standing by her, when she knows you are willing to do things that make you uncomfortable, she is better equipped to take care of herself and the growing baby. Both of you will feel surges of elation and fatigue as the baby's due date draws nearer, so having a birth plan in place (which we will cover later on) will keep everyone well-balanced.

Prepare for the Blitz

Kirsten told me she was pregnant with Grace in the summer of 2008. Nine months later, in the wee hours of the morning, I timed Kirsten's contractions while she sat up in bed, and we realized it was time. I threw our meticulously packed bags into the car and sped off to the hospital. Movies like to portray deliveries in cars, with fraught husbands catching their newborns like footballs, or men being pulled over by the police while their pregnant wife screams like a woman possessed. In our case, life imitated art: I was pulled over for speeding, even though I was not, and the officer proceeded to shine his bright flashlight at me, my wife, and her pregnant belly. He gave me a rather callous, "Well, get to the hospital then." We were as calm as possible—no screaming, no tantrums, because that wouldn't solve anything—plus time was of the essence!

The point is, unexpected events happen even when you have a plan, but staying calm and acting reasonably can easily tip the balance between a horror story and a cute anecdote. When that baby is ready, all that will register in your mind is: *Game time!*

At the hospital, time seemed to move more slowly than it did before we conceived. My wife labored for hours, and there isn't an NFL workout that compares to the experience. I had been to classes and watched videos on the delivery process, and despite all my preparation, I felt helpless yet awestruck by how strong and in control she was during such a chaotic and agonizing ordeal. I had no idea how hard the labor was going to be on *me*—and I know that sounds bad. I'm six foot three and 250 pounds, and what my tiny wife was doing right then made my head spin. Then I heard Grace's first wail, and fear was replaced by blinding joy.

After Grace was born and we were together in the hospital room, I removed my shirt and pressed my baby girl to my chest. I acted on instinct. It is typical for the baby to be placed on the mother's chest immediately following birth to regulate the heartbeat and to establish an instant bond. Men can do this too, and it is bliss. Later in the day, after Kirsten fed Grace a few times, I had the opportunity to do skin-to-skin bonding again.

Time becomes foggy when you are home bonding with your new family. I hope this book will help prepare you for the major life changes heading your way. Parenting changes you like little else.

Parents joke about how caring for a newborn transforms you into a zombie and that you never sleep again—and in those first few weeks and months, you believe it. Guess what— you adapt. Commitment makes you a better person, and this book will show you how to hold the line, even when the blitz is on.

Being Present

Be sure to pull your load in those weeks following delivery— cook, clean, do laundry. It sounds simple, but remember, you will probably continue working outside of the home, and you are not just there to provide a roof over your family's head—you need to take care of the people inside it too.

Some men aren't prepared to become fathers. I understand that. Some grew up in fatherless households or without a decent role model, and feel unequipped when they find out they're having a baby. I wrote this book for the guy who doesn't think he's ready to become a father and, whether he

28

admits it or not, fears the challenges and the unknown. That covers a lot of men, whether they planned the pregnancy or not. The point is, once a man knows there's a baby coming and understands what that baby needs, I think he will care about the kind of home life he establishes, and he will take on greater responsibility raising that child. Children need their fathers to be part of their lives, and if men comprehend this, I'm sure they will be spurred on to develop into the men they thought they weren't ready to become.

This book explains the terms men will hear during prenatal visits to the doctor, and how the baby develops in the womb. I will also discuss what to expect when your wife changes and how to handle those changes. This way, you'll understand exactly what's happening at every stage of the pregnancy and delivery process. I think this book will please the woman in your life as well, especially if she has experienced the lack of a male presence in raising a child before. More information means less fear and more confidence in your abilities to be an excellent father. Remember, you are building a legacy, and this book can help.

The day your wife pulls out a Superman onesie to announce you are having a boy, or the day you dress your baby girl in her first Easter dress—these are life's most precious moments and memories. To use the language of the gridiron, this book will take you through training camp, regular season, Super Bowl, postgame, and off-season. You will warm up, try out some of the drills, learn the playbook; you will lift weights and run. You'll do all of it. Dads are smart. You can do this. You *need* to do this. Let's get started.

CHAPTER TWO

Pre-practice Warm-Up

What *You* Should Expect
When *She's* Expecting

Pregnancy can be very lonely for both men and women. Some women claim men become aloof and distant, while men feel that their wives become different people, alienating them from the process. To keep this from happening to you, use this time to remind your wife that you're thinking about her. Tell her she's beautiful, fix her a snack, and say, "I love you." These are a few ways you can show her you've got her back.

Many men instinctively want to fix things—leaky faucets, wobbly desks, and sometimes even their spouses. This is especially true when a woman is pregnant. Unfortunately, there's no "fixing" pregnancy, but there are ways to make this ten-month adventure easier, all while maintaining your sanity. In this chapter, I will share my own experiences with loneliness during pregnancy and offer tips to help men navigate this exciting time in their lives. Most importantly, I'll cover how to help out so that you don't feel left out.

Fear Factor: Keeping It Together

When a woman finds out she's pregnant, the news is momentous, but all the excitement and joy can quickly turn to fear. With hormones flying, responsibilities multiplying, baby items overflowing, it's no wonder a lot of relationships fall apart when a woman is expecting. I've seen it happen more often than I'd like to admit—men hear "baby" and bolt. This is the time to step up your commitment, and a little effort will go a long way toward sustaining and strengthening a meaningful relationship.

I've worked alongside athletes whose girlfriends get pregnant, and I ask if they're planning on getting married. "Well, I don't know. What's the point?" they say. "We're living together, and I'm making enough money to take care of the child. That's enough."

It's not enough. These guys are afraid of commitment. Often they don't want to leave their girlfriends, but they're not willing to get married. They think that financial security is all a child needs. That's just not true.

There's a reason why having children out of wedlock has long been taboo—a marriage provides security for everyone involved, and not just financially. Virtually every culture on earth and across time has recognized this; it's even why governments promote marriage.

Married couples, and married couples with kids, are treated differently for tax purposes—that's why tax forms ask if you are married and have children. Married couples can own real property in many states in a way that provides additional legal protection. Married couples have inheritance rights that unmarried couples may not have. Married couples may have additional insurance benefits. So there are financial reasons and legal reasons, but there is another important reason: emotional stability.

Studies show that marriage provides greater emotional, financial, and health benefits than just living together, and married couples are better equipped to raise healthy, emotionally stable children.[1] Marriage benefits all of society, and that's why many cultures, religions, and even governments take steps to promote marriage. Now, that doesn't mean that all marriages last forever—people get divorced—but it's more difficult to run away from a marriage than it is from a long-term relationship. Some men get it. Others don't want to get it. So guys, when your girl tells you she's pregnant, put a ring on it. Better yet, put the ring on *before* she gets pregnant!

Listen to Her, Don't Fix Her

As I mentioned earlier, men want to fix things, but when a woman is pregnant, she really needs her husband to listen to her. That means you should learn her needs and attend to them. Remember the story about Kirsten's morning sickness? Here's the rest of the story, and it demonstrates how you can serve your wife by observing her.

When Kirsten was pregnant with our first child, we went on a quick getaway to the Caribbean. It was July, and training camp was right around the corner. Kirsten was still in her first trimester, and we were a bundle of nerves. One morning I woke up expecting to head down to the beach for a day of

33

rest and relaxation, but as I headed to the bathroom, I saw Kirsten, kneeling in front of the toilet and retching, sicker than I'd ever seen her. This was uncharted territory for both of us, but instead of asking her questions and trying to figure out how to fix the situation, I came up behind her, pulled her hair back, and held her as she vomited into the basin.

At the time, I didn't think it was such a big deal—in all honesty, I didn't know what else to do. But since then, whenever Kirsten talks about her first pregnancy, that's the story that comes up the most. It was exactly what she needed at that moment. She didn't need me to find a solution to a problem—morning sickness happens—nor did she have the strength to tell me that she needed help. I assessed the situation and helped her manage her pain without her having to tell me to do it. It doesn't sound like much, but gestures like that can make a woman feel like you're there for her and that she's not alone during her pregnancy.

For some men, listening does not come naturally. We've got to practice listening, and by learning that skill, we open new opportunities for productive dialogue. To do that, we need to study our wives and learn what they need. Ask yourself: Is your wife an introvert or an extrovert? How does she handle pain? What's the best thing you can do for her in the heat of the moment? Sometimes a little common sense goes a long way.

When I held Kirsten that morning in the hotel bathroom, I didn't know whether it was the right thing to do, and I certainly didn't run through a playbook of possible scenarios, but I knew that she needed support, and holding her was what I could provide. Rather than say, "I know how you feel," because you don't, be willing to take a supporting role. It can make all the difference.

Here's another example that shows how gestures can help your spouse and strengthen your relationship. Kirsten used to eat a small, protein-packed snack when she woke up in the morning, otherwise she'd feel nauseous. Knowing this, I would prepare peanut butter on toast for her before I headed to practice in the morning. I left a plate by her bedside within arm's reach. It wasn't much, but it curbed her morning sickness, and I had contributed to her well-being.

Even as the pregnancy progresses, remember that you are partners in this endeavor, and maintaining contact is crucial. Don't stop doing the fun things you used to do together—take walks, cook dinner, and visit friends. Your wife may want to nest as soon as she finds out a baby is on the way, but encourage her to get out of the house and get moving.

Be sure your doctor gives her the green light on moderate exercise first. Pregnancy is not the time to start an exercise program, but if your wife was active before conceiving, her doctor might encourage her to continue. This is also a good time to research pediatricians and hospitals and enroll in birthing classes. Go to these appointments with her—you'll establish connections with fellow local parents-to-be while strengthening your role as a father and husband.

The Loneliness of Pregnancy

Many women experience a sense of loneliness, especially with the first pregnancy. Something else is taking control of their bodies—hormones, morning sickness, fatigue, and emotional spikes all play a role in that. I remember Kirsten would cry for what seemed like no reason. She would bawl, unable to stop herself, nor really explain what set her off in the first place. A sad movie scene, recalling a tender memory, or an act of kindness could get the tears flowing. It was confusing for both of us. She couldn't tell me why she was was crying, and I couldn't figure it out either.

This is uncharted territory for first-time mothers, and some women encounter loneliness during subsequent pregnancies. Husbands need to be mindful of this and try to be sensitive to their spouse's feelings. Making a joke at your wife's expense will not help. Offering tissues and a glass of water, on the other hand, can be one of those critical gestures that shows her you care, that you are there for her, and that you are a team.

Sometimes loneliness can indicate a more serious problem, and you need to be aware of that as well. The American Pregnancy Association estimates that between 14 and 23 percent of women exhibit symptoms of depression during pregnancy. Below are some of the signs of depression during pregnancy that you should look for:

- Difficulty concentrating
- Sleeping too little or too much
- Recurring thoughts of death, suicide, or hopelessness
- Anxiety
- Feelings of guilt and worthlessness
- Change in eating habits[2]

If your wife experiences any of these symptoms for more than two weeks, call her doctor so that you can get professional advice. A depressed mother often lacks the strength to care for a newborn, and babies with depressed mothers may be more prone to developmental issues, so early diagnosis and treatment are critical.

Languages of Love

Let's talk about love languages. I bet you've never heard of them, but I think they're a powerful tool in bonding and communicating with your wife. Relationship counselor and author Gary Chapman explores them in his 1995 bestseller, *The Five Love Languages*. In it, he says there are five ways to express commitment to your loved one, and that each of us experiences love differently. The five ways in which we express and experience love include the following:

- Giving or receiving gifts
- Spending quality time
- Words of affirmation
- Acts of devotion
- Intimacy

First, find out which language applies to your wife. Perhaps your wife needs to hear words of affirmation—that no matter what she looks like, she's still beautiful to you. Other women appreciate gifts. Let's go through the different love languages so that you can determine exactly what your wife needs. As you read, you may find that your wife requires a combination of love languages, and you may also realize that some of these gifts apply to you as well. Don't forget about these languages after the baby arrives: you will need to remind each other of your love when you're caring for the newborn.

Love Language One: Words of Affirmation

Kirsten and I have been blessed with five children, all currently under the age of eight. My wife is a full-time, stay-at-home mother, a homeschool teacher, and a participant in charitable work as well. Since I'm at work every day, Kirsten spends most days shouldering the day-to-day management of the household, and it's a lot of work.

I know that the best thing I can do is say, "You are doing a great job taking care of the kids and this house. You're raising a wonderful family. You are a great mother and wife." These declarations are verbal gifts. I've learned that showering Kirsten with praise, especially when the going gets tough, reminds her that our family is worth the effort.

Sometimes saying something as simple as "Thank you" in the middle of a hectic and frenzied day is the perfect cure for a bad mood. If your marriage is faltering or you aren't communicating as much as before a baby came into the picture, try a few words of appreciation.

Remember the old adage "You catch more flies with honey than with vinegar." If your wife seems out of sorts, she may just need to hear a few love-affirming words, reminding her that you love her and that she is doing important work—bringing your baby into the world. False praise, however, is cheap, and your wife will likely know you don't mean it. So don't do that, because it will make her feel worse than if you had said nothing at all.

Love Language Two: Gifts

While some women appreciate a well-timed word (or two) of encouragement, others appreciate a well-timed present. Don't read this wrong: gifts need not break the bank. It really is the thought that counts, and for some women, this is how they need to be loved. A gift may be a bouquet of flowers, a day at the spa, or lunch from her favorite restaurant. Women may feel especially vulnerable during pregnancy, and a gesture like this goes a long way to reassuring them that they're doing a great job.

Love Language Three: Quality Time

Perhaps your wife loves nothing more than having your undivided attention. This is a wonderful love language, but for some men, giving this gift is easier said than done. Think about breakfast: You and your wife are sitting in the breakfast nook. The television is on, maybe there's a newspaper or magazine open, and of course, the cell phone is within arm's reach. Are all of these distractions in front of you?

Take a look at your wife—is she just mushing her cereal around, staring? She may be waiting for a moment to have a conversation—about the weather, the baby, dinner—it doesn't matter. What does matter is that she needs your attention at that particular moment, and she doesn't want to compete with the television, newspaper, magazine, or cell phone.

Here's the hard part. You have to turn off the television, close your magazine, put down the paper, move the phone to another room (don't just slip it into your pocket), and listen to your wife. Look at her while you're having a conversation, and you'll be amazed at how profoundly this will improve her mood and outlook on the pregnancy.

Love Language Four: Gifts of Intimacy

Many of you reading this are probably thinking this is an easy gift to fulfill. Not necessarily. A gift of intimacy doesn't always imply sex. It might be a light touch on your wife's shoulder, holding hands, or a massage. Sex is another powerful form of physical intimacy.

Every woman has different needs that change over the course of nine months. During pregnancy, some women love to have their growing bellies caressed, and others experience a surge in sexual desire. Be attuned to her needs, and act accordingly. It's important not to judge your wife—saying something like, "Wow, your belly is huge!" won't earn you many bonus points. An expectant mother who revels in gifts of intimacy needs your touch, not nasty or sarcastic remarks at her expense.

Love Language Five: Gifts of Devotion

Gifts of devotion, or acts of service, are another way to love your wife. Some women don't mind being told they're loved, but what they'd really like is for their husbands to do the dishes, walk the dog, fold the laundry, or install the car seat. Some of you may feel this is just a way for your wife to get extra work out of you while she puts up her feet. Sure, you put in a long day in the workplace (or on the gridiron), but for a woman whose primary love language is acts of service, you need to show that you're committed to the relationship by pulling your weight.

Do keep in mind that pregnant women shouldn't engage in certain forms of physical labor (like painting or lifting heavy objects), and you ought to be helping out anyway, but don't let this language lapse after the baby arrives. Changing a diaper (which we'll discuss in a future chapter) so she can get ten extra minutes of sleep, fixing formula, or tidying around the house will be greatly appreciated.

How do you figure out which gift your wife appreciates most? Study her needs and desires, and get giving. Try them and see what works most for her. Pregnancy is as joyous as it is hectic, and it's important to remind your wife that your love is strong.

When Hormones Start Flying, Stay Cool

During these nine months, arguments can occur over seemingly insignificant issues, and they can get heated. At one point early in Kirsten's pregnancy, she was feeling down. I wanted to talk to her about something, but she didn't want to listen. I admit I got mad. I thought, *The baby's taking over our relationship already!* I got selfish and made the pregnancy about me. I huffed for a while, then took a few deep breaths and reassessed the situation.

It's hard to be rational when you're in the scrum, but there are a few techniques (like breathing slowly) that help. I find that deep breaths and exercise are great ways to blow off steam. Pump some iron, pound the pavement, toss the pigskin, and in twenty minutes you won't remember why you were so upset. It's also important to have another mature man in your life from whom you can receive wise counsel. Iron sharpens iron.

Every time Kirsten and I have been blessed with another pregnancy, I get sad and even lonely—I feel like I'm losing my wife for a while. I'm used to having open and honest communication with Kirsten, but sometimes, during her pregnancies, she just can't provide that same level of interaction, and I'm frustrated because there's little I can do that will take the discomfort away completely. We know each other so well at this point that she's comfortable telling me that even though she's not interacting with me the same way as before, we're still on the same team. Remember that. You may hear "I'm just tired, and I want to go to sleep right now" or "I don't want to talk." Even "I don't want to have sex right now." It's not personal—she's carrying a little life inside her, after all—and don't let that get in the way of the big game.

Your needs, though important, aren't the top priority right now. It takes two to make a baby, and your contribution is significant, but these few months are (mostly) about her. So she may take nesting or decorating the baby's nursery to an obsessive level of detail, and you might get caught in the crosshairs. Don't sweat it. You've got this.

Pregnancy, Training Camp–Style

Pregnancy is a lot like training camp. It's rigorous, exhilarating yet exhausting, and you don't see the fruits of your labor for months. Think of your baby's arrival as the Super Bowl. It's exciting, and everyone is on edge for the big day to arrive. In reality, it takes nine months of pain and hard work to reach delivery day. She might think she regrets her decision—and you might feel the same. It's normal, but you have to push through the tough times. Using some of the techniques I mentioned above will help.

Think about the situations where you've wanted to quit, and when your wife was there to pick you up, brush the dust off you, and send you back out. Early in my career there was a time when I was ready to throw in the towel. In 2004, I was playing for the New England Patriots. I remember being in preseason training, and it was grueling. At the end of each day, I would call Kirsten, saying I couldn't do it anymore, that I was ready to come home. She reminded me that I could push through, and that she would support me every step of the way. Of course, she was right. (We won the Super Bowl that year too.)

Pregnancy is similar. There will be times when your wife will doubt her abilities, worry if the baby will be healthy, and wonder if all this change and sacrifice is worth it. And you have to remind her that the end result—your child—is worth it.

Benjamin Watson: Super Bowl Champion, Pro Cheerleader

If pregnancy is like training camp, then you need to be your wife's cheerleader. As much as you may want to play a larger role in your wife's pregnancy, biology simply won't allow it. Meanwhile, your wife's body is going through amazing changes during this time. I think it's beautiful that a woman can adapt and nurture another life, but I also can't imagine going through childbirth. I am happy to be the cheerleader, and that's what Kirsten needs when she's pregnant.

Your wife needs you to be in her corner too. This can be difficult for a lot of men. Think about the guys in my profession. NFL players are used to hearing fans cheer and offer accolades, and they certainly aren't used to handing out compliments. You may not be a professional football player, but I'm willing to bet that if you're talented at your job, you're used to people telling you how great you are. Your wife needs to hear that. Positive affirmation is a form of security. I learned this through trial and error. Here's how I learned to be Kirsten's cheerleader.

In the early months of her first pregnancy, I remember wondering why Kirsten didn't treat me the same way my fans did, and I asked her about it. It was a quick conversation. "I'm not your fan. I'm your wife, and I'm your friend," she responded. "And right now, I'm carrying our child." Enough said.

We have to be able to differentiate between fans and family, and that can be very difficult to do, even if you don't play professional football. One of the major reasons husbands and wives fight is because women treat their husbands differently than everyone else—they know exactly what makes their men tick and what ticks them off. Your bond should be so strong that you don't need false praise. Providing strength and encouragement is one thing; unnecessary flattery is a false form of cheerleading. Be sure you recognize the difference, because your wife will.

Be Present

In our society, men are often encouraged to step aside when a woman is pregnant. We hear, "It's women's work" or "You're in the way; we'll call you when we're done." Many men are fine with being pushed aside during pregnancy, and in previous generations that was acceptable. Now, more men would prefer to have a greater role in the process; they just don't know how.

Men aren't in the way if they're doing the right thing. We're not fish, fertilizing eggs and then swimming away. Men should be involved in their children's lives, from conception to adulthood. For the moment, accept that there will be some things you just aren't good at—at least, not right away. Have you ever changed a diaper? Practice makes perfect. Learn how to prepare breast milk or formula for late-night feedings. Select the books you'll read to your baby. Be willing to learn and take direction, and soon enough you will feel like an equal partner again.

Some men may feel that listening and taking direction from their wives is a subordinate role. Yes, your roles have changed, but you are still important. She's not walking behind you, and you're not walking behind her. You are equal partners in parenthood; just keep in mind that the dynamics of leadership have changed. You are still a leader, but you are leading by serving the needs of your wife.

What does that mean for you? As a husband and father, your job is to love your wife, and that means making a decision to devote your life to her and to your child. Right now that might mean making some extra room in bed for that special pillow your wife got to make her more comfortable at night. Or it might mean fixing her a plate of peanut butter toast. Service, not chest-beating, is the way to lead, love, and inspire.

Playing Defense

When family and friends find out you're expecting, be prepared for an onslaught of self-proclaimed experts offering advice on everything from feeding times to proper burping techniques. At a time when some women feel isolated in their own bodies, they're hearing all sorts of advice, much of it unsolicited. I imagine it's like having an out-of-body experience in front of an audience.

Your role during all this is to be your wife's offensive lineman, protecting her ears and her heart from the blitzing onslaught of opinions. Don't be a nightclub bouncer. Don't kick people out of your lives, but be on the lookout for folks who, however well-intentioned, may scare your wife with horrible delivery stories or who offer bad medical advice. Leave the medical advice to the doctor. Your wife may not be emotionally prepared for this, so it's your job to say, "Hold on. Just because something happened to one person doesn't mean it's going to happen here. What's the point in scaring my wife?"

Your wife may usually be able to fend off such chatter, but the emotional intensity of pregnancy may throw her off her game, making it essential for you to step up and play defense. It may be a little uncomfortable for you to do this, especially if this unsolicited advice is coming from close friends or family, but there's no need to be confrontational or nasty. Keep your blocking game clean. You're protecting your quarterback here, but you don't want a flag thrown for a personal foul.

If a friend is obviously making your wife uncomfortable, simply say, "Thanks for your concern, but if that happens to us, we'll consult a doctor." Then change the subject to something less stressful, like favorite baby books or nursery decorations.

Just as it's important to filter negative influences, make sure your wife is surrounded by people who bring positive energy. Ask your wife who she wants to be around her—as much as she may love your mother, she may not be comfortable having her over every day, no matter how well-intentioned the visits are. Encourage her to spend time with people who will provide love and emotional support without adding extra baggage.

Birth Plans and Sharing the Happy News

Having your own birth plan ensures that you and your wife understand each other and what to expect during pregnancy and delivery. Again, plenty of people will offer their own ideas on childbirth, which may contradict your own beliefs. It's much easier to decline such advice when you've already got a solid game plan in place. Talk to your doctor together and decide on a plan. A sample birth plan may include the following:

- Who you want to be present during delivery, including family, friends, or children
- Whether you plan to stay in bed or be mobile during labor
- Preferred birthing positions (walking, squatting, lying down)
- Pain management options
- Preferred modes of hydration

Keep your birth plan short—one page is perfect—and tape it to the fridge. It will ease a lot of stress and provide peace of mind. Delivery day may go off-script at the last moment, but your birth plan should cover various possible outcomes.[3]

It's not up to you alone to decide when to tell friends and family you're having a baby. Make that decision together. I know plenty of guys who start sharing the news with their buddies, and their wives have no clue. I think that's a mistake. There's nothing more awkward than running into friends who congratulate you when your wife isn't aware that they know.

Kirsten and I waited until she was twelve weeks pregnant before we shared our news, and we talked about who we wanted to know first, and when. That meant staying off social media. Telling friends you are having a baby but saying, "Don't tell your wife" is a disservice to your wife and to your matrimonial bond. Although you may be so excited that you want to scream from the rafters, remember that your wife trusts you, so check with her first.

Finding Out the Baby's Sex and Planning for the Unexpected

Kirsten and I are planners. We like to have as much information as possible before making an informed decision, and that was especially true when it came to learning our baby's sex. We've always found out so that there wouldn't be any surprises. Some parents really want a boy or a girl, and if the baby happens to be the opposite of what you were hoping for, finding out early lets you come to terms with those feelings, which are normal and natural.

It happened to me—I really wanted our first child to be a boy, but I didn't want to find out in the delivery room that we were having a girl. Kirsten and I asked the doctor to write down the sex on a slip of paper, and we read it when we got home. When it turned out that our firstborn would be a girl, I admit it, I felt disappointed. I was thinking about playing catch and all those other special things that fathers and sons share. I even thought, *Well, we're going to try again, because I really want a boy.* But since we found out early, I had my private pity party, and when I saw my daughter Grace for the first time, I was in heaven.

During our second pregnancy, I was more nervous than the first time. We had another girl. Kirsten said my face just dropped, and she felt totally alone because I was disappointed at the baby's sex. I'm not proud of it, but that's how I felt. I moped for quite a while, but then I finally got over it. Looking back, I can't imagine having it any other way. Our girls are beautiful, kind, and help look after their younger brothers. As always, God knew what he was doing.

Even though I didn't have the boys first, I'm thankful for the girls being the oldest. It was still difficult to accept, so my advice is this: whether you find out or not is your decision, but be aware of how your reaction might upset your wife. My disappointment really spoke to Kirsten. Being distraught over the baby's sex wasn't the best way for me to support her and love her. Try and remember that a healthy baby is the best baby. (And you can still play catch with girls.)

CHAPTER THREE

What's in a Name and Babymoons

What's in a Name? A Lot

Most couples have a formula for choosing a name. A couple I know had their child's name picked out years before they were even married. They were sitting at a bar one night, and the song "Leila" came on the stereo. "If we ever have a baby, we're going to name her Leila," they said to each other. Sure enough, a decade later, they had a baby girl and named her Leila.

I'm sure their story is familiar—we all know couples who are fond of a particular name. Kirsten and I wanted our children to have names that were spiritually meaningful, names that made us smile and spoke truth to our children and to us when we said them. Kirsten had the girls' names picked out before I knew we were having a baby. She chose Grace for our oldest daughter. At first I thought the name sounded

51

old-fashioned, but when Kirsten explained her rationale, I couldn't love it more.

We looked up Ephesians 2:8 and 9: "For it is by grace you have been saved, through faith—and this is not from yourselves, it is the gift of God." We had the verse painted on the nursery wall, and it reminds us of God's unmerited favor credited to us because of the shed blood of his Son. Grace's middle name is Makayla, which means "Who is like the Lord?" Nobody, of course. What a reminder.

Kirsten had our second daughter's name selected too—Naomi—because she loves the story of Naomi, which appears in the book of Ruth in the Bible. The name means "sweet," "pleasant," or "Joy of Jehovah," and her story shows how God's benevolence has the power to coax good fortune out of bitter situations. Naomi's middle name is Love. I had nothing to do with that, but Kirsten smiled every time she said it. It's got a great high-fashion ring to it. I think she's going to be famous with that name!

Before she even knew she was pregnant with our third daughter, Kirsten had been reading through the Bible and finished it in a year. In Genesis, the first book of the Bible, God placed the first man and woman in the Garden of Eden. It was a perfect paradise where God walked with his creation in the cool of the day. Although Kirsten had read the account before, Eden had never resonated as a potential baby name until then. When we found out we were having a girl, the first name was set. Her middle name, Moriah, came to me while I was in the middle of a workout! Moriah was the name of the mountain where God provided Abraham a ram to take his son Isaac's place on the altar. When I think of this name, I am reminded of God's provision and faithfulness in keeping his promises.

We chose the boys' names together. Isaiah's name means "God is salvation," and every time I call him, I am reminded that God alone can save. Judah means "God be praised." The boys' middle names are variations on my name: Isaiah's middle name is Benjamin, and Judah's middle name is the same as mine, Seth.

Whatever your motivation for selecting a name, remember that the name will last the child's entire life (unless they change it). I would advise against choosing a trendy name or an overly complicated name or one that has the potential to be embarrassing. A name that sounds cute now might seem juvenile in adulthood.

Once you have a name in mind, repeat it out loud and write it down. Imagine your child as an adult, carrying the name you chose. You may not be 100 percent sure it's the right one, but you'll know immediately if it's the wrong one. Sometimes I would spend the weeks following my children's birth wondering if we had chosen the right names for them. There was always a close second choice that kept me wavering. But eventually all the names grew on me because I loved their meanings.

Babymoons

You've heard of honeymoons, and maybe you went on one when you got married. Now some couples take "babymoons" when they find out they're having a child. It's a relaxing, sometimes romantic vacation, often taken in the first or second trimester, and it's a great way to enjoy time together before the baby arrives.

There's a point during the third trimester when women are discouraged from traveling long distances or flying, but

Kirsten and I didn't take that advice. She was nine months pregnant when we took our babymoon. It was a quick trip—Boston to New York—only three hours down the highway, and Kirsten didn't even look like she was about to have a child, so we got away with that one.

As I mentioned in chapter 1, Grace was born on January 31, 2009. That also happened to be the year the New England Patriots didn't go to the playoffs (even though we were 11–5!), so I knew I would be by Kirsten's side in the delivery room. But before delivery day, Kirsten and I decided that we wanted to go to Times Square and see the ball drop on New Year's Eve—admittedly, not the most relaxing venue. It was close to her due date, but I'm glad we spent that time together. If I were to do it again, I would consider planning our trip earlier in her pregnancy—it's hard to do a lot of activities with a woman who's about to give birth.

I think babymoons are a great way to spend quality time together, and it reaffirms your marital bond. The trip doesn't have to be fancy—don't break the bank—but even a long weekend at a hotel in the city provides time together, and it's probably the last time in a long time that your lives will be this simple.

Babymoons are a time to relax, because soon enough you'll be facing long nights, early mornings, and plenty of dirty diapers. Even if your wife is hesitant about booking a babymoon, try to convince her otherwise; it will be a nice memory to cherish after the pregnancy is over.

Although I prefer babymoons with just the two of us, this doesn't always have to be the case. Before our fourth child, we went with another couple to Puerto Rico. As a group, we spent mornings relaxing together and evenings at dinner and local events. A babymoon can even be a solo affair. Take the kids for a night or two and send your wife to a local hotel to rest, recharge, and order room service. This is especially helpful when other children are already part of the family. This was the best option for us before number five arrived. It was difficult for us to find time to get away together, but a night away from kid duties does wonders for the psyche. It's important for mom to be as rested as possible, mentally and physically, before the strain of labor and birth.

CHAPTER FOUR

Sex

The Good, the Bad, and Everything in Between

Let's Talk about (No) Sex

Intimacy is a hot topic, and I'm not just talking about sex. Your wife will crave emotional intimacy during pregnancy, and that may mean spending more time at home and less time at happy hour. You may be pleasantly surprised and find yourself enjoying this nesting phase. This is how you build trust between each other, and that trust will sustain and strengthen your relationship long after the baby arrives.

Men need to be honest about their needs regarding sex. Guys worry that their spouses won't want to be physically intimate anymore, and it's a major factor in why men stray during a pregnancy. Whether your wife wants to have sex or not, you must have that discussion with her. Be honest about what you need and how you're going to get through the pregnancy. There can be a happy medium, but you'll never find it if you don't communicate with each other.

If you feel uncomfortable about having that conversation, then consider finding spiritual guidance or other outside counsel. Sometimes an impartial listener makes it easier to talk about such delicate subjects, but don't avoid the conversation for fear of being embarrassed. Frustration is worse, and talking it out will help. You'll get through it, and your bond will be stronger for your efforts.

Sex and Pregnancy: Let Her Initiate

Women's bodies change during pregnancy, and that includes huge shifts in hormones and sex drive. During the first trimester, many women experience morning sickness, mood swings, and dips in energy. They're generally feeling a lot better during the second trimester, and the sex drive comes back. Before Kirsten was ever pregnant, I remember a Patriots teammate talking about his wife's third pregnancy. "It's the first trimester, and it's rough," he said to me. "But I can't wait for the second trimester, because it's on!"

Okay, so that might not be you, but believe me when I say that everything changes. As I mentioned in chapter 2, your wife may not be interested in sex right now, but that could change with the arrival of the second trimester. Some women feel incredibly sexy during pregnancy, and others would rather hide under the sheets for nine months. Everyone is different.

For Kirsten and I, the second trimester was the sweet spot. The lights came back on. She had that sparkle in her eye again, and I felt like I had my wife back. Kirsten wanted to go out, and she was her radiant, happy self again. When the third trimester rolls around, many women can barely find comfortable positions for sleeping, let alone for sex. If your wife is still in the first trimester and you're feeling frustrated, remember that she will come back to you. It might seem like she has become another person and some tiny creature has taken over her body, but give it time. She'll be back.

As a rule of thumb, don't even ask your wife about sex during the first trimester. Let her initiate. She'll let you know when she wants to be intimate. Don't take my word for it—that's advice straight from Kirsten! Expect to provide early morning snacks and foot massages for the first twelve weeks, but by the second trimester, most morning sickness is gone and women are feeling better.

Here's a pro tip: make your wife feel sexy even when she doesn't think she is; she'll feel better and want to be intimate with you. Be careful, however, about using gifts as a rationale for sex. She won't be pleased if you try to pressure her into sex with a quid pro quo like, "I gave you a great weekend at a spa. What are you going to give me?" In my experience, even when she's not feeling well, my wife has been incredibly and sacrificially in tune to my needs in this area. Our willingness and freedom to communicate honestly in this area grew with each pregnancy.

Pregnancy and Infidelity

One of the biggest fears women have during pregnancy is infidelity. It's not as uncommon as you may think. While pregnancy can bring a couple closer, it can also trigger men to cheat on their wives. Understandably, there isn't a lot of hard data on the topic—few women want to talk about infidelity and their husbands—and even fewer men feel comfortable admitting their misstep.

In his infinite wisdom, God made men and women to complement each other. Generally speaking, sex strengthens emotional intimacy for men, while emotional intimacy increases sexual desire for women. Consequently, when men can't have as much sex during their wife's pregnancy as before, sometimes they feel rejected and alone. Some men can't see over this blip on the sexual radar, thinking that this lack of physical sexual intimacy will continue after the baby arrives. And although your wife won't be able to hop right into bed with you after she delivers the baby, your relationship can endure.

How can you avoid cheating on your wife? Being intimate doesn't always mean having sex. Couples massage and sensual touching are other ways to maintain emotional and physical contact. A touch on the small of the back, or a simple embrace around the belly, sealed with a kiss on the neck is always more important than intercourse, not only now but through all stages of relationships. Holding hands in public, opening doors, and offering words of affirmation are all key ingredients to healthy intimacy. Be willing to communicate too. Tell your wife how you're feeling. If you can't talk to her or don't know how to engage in this conversation, a therapist may be able to provide guidance and counsel. And remember, the easiest way to avoid something is to become consumed with something else. Life is not simply about avoiding the bad. It is about chasing the good. By pursuing what's right, we leave little time or space for what could destroy our lives and break up our relationships. By pursuing your wife and her needs, you will inevitably tighten your focus and strengthen your allegiance to her and to your growing family.

PART 2

REGULAR SEASON

CHAPTER FIVE

X's and O's

Your Pregnancy Handbook

So, your wife took a pregnancy test, and it's positive. Now what? We explored how your relationship with your wife changes in the previous chapter. Here, we're going to get technical.

You may have heard the terms *placenta*, *uterus*, and *fetus*, but do you know what they mean? Why is it important to know these words, anyway?

Understanding pregnancy terminology is empowering for men—it's another way we can be a part of the process. It can also help you have greater awareness of the changes going on with your wife and baby, understand the doctors during medical appointments, and keep track of your child's development.

As a football player, I'm used to body trauma, and when a part of my body doesn't feel right, I want to know what's causing the issue. I feel the same way about pregnancy—I want to know all about it so that if something isn't right, my wife and I can address it. I also think the pregnancy process is beautiful—everything happening to your wife's body is for a reason, and I believe that knowledge boosts confidence.

Are you ready to go back to health class? Don't worry, this class is easy. We're not going to cover six years of medical school in one chapter. Instead, I'm going to give you the basics, and with these basics, you'll be ready for game day.

Being prepared shows your wife you're interested and involved. Imagine, for example, that you are at the doctor's office and he says something you don't understand. Don't be intimidated—ask for an explanation. Not only will you learn something important regarding your wife and unborn child, you'll also show your wife that you are an active partner she can rely on.

I'll be throwing some technical language your way too. Don't sweat it if you weren't the science kid in high school. This won't be as tough as you think—you've got this. We'll talk about what exactly pregnancy is and how the baby develops over the course of nine months, as well as fitness, nutrition, and financial considerations that arise as a result of having children. Important terms are *italicized* and defined throughout.

Ready? Here we go. A pregnancy is divided into *trimesters*—three distinct phases of development where the baby and your wife undergo major changes. We're going to look at each one. Let's start with the first trimester.

First Trimester: Weeks 1–12

About three weeks after a woman has her *menstrual cycle* (her period), the body prepares for *ovulation*, when the ovary releases an egg into the *fallopian tube* (the duct the egg travels through), where it waits to be fertilized. Millions of sperm enter the vagina after a man ejaculates. They travel up the fallopian tube, and it only takes one to make a baby.

Conception is when one sperm enters an egg, creating a *zygote*. Even though most women don't realize they're pregnant yet, features like hair color, eye color, and sex have already been determined—it's all in your genes! Though sex was determined the instant the zygote was created, medical science is way behind nature—you won't be able to find out whether the baby is a boy or girl until about twenty weeks into the pregnancy. Each zygote contains forty-six *chromosomes*. These are rod-shaped structures that carry DNA, and the baby receives twenty-three from the sperm and twenty-three from the egg.

Once the zygote is formed, it travels farther down the fallopian tube into the *uterus*, a hollow organ that the baby will call home until being born. The zygote attaches to the walls of the uterus. Then the zygote forms into many cells. The cell at the middle of this pack is called the *embryo*—this is what will develop into your baby. The other cells surrounding the embryo will stick tightly to the uterus, which is already lined thick with blood to support the development of a baby.

This all occurs within approximately three weeks of conception. At this point, your baby's brain, heart, and gastrointestinal tract have already begun development—all in that tiny embryo, which is the size of the period at the end of this sentence.

A woman generally finds out she is pregnant during weeks four through seven, and this is also when she may experience symptoms of early pregnancy, such as breast tenderness and lower backaches. Nausea and increased sensitivity to smell and taste are common signs of morning sickness. Unfortunately, morning sickness doesn't just happen in the morning; it can happen at any time of the day and varies from pregnancy to pregnancy. Kirsten suffered extreme bouts of morning sickness and vomiting with the first two babies but only endured mild nausea for the last three.

The following are some ways your wife can manage the symptoms of morning sickness:

- Avoid spicy food.
- Eat small meals rather than large meals, but don't skip meals either.
- Take a daily B6 vitamin, which has been shown to reduce symptoms of morning sickness.
- Don't lie down after eating.
- Smell ginger or lemons—the scent helps ease nausea.
- Drink lemonade or ginger ale, or eat watermelon—they help reduce nausea too.
- Consult your doctor about prescribing supplements to manage morning sickness.

Since certain smells trigger morning sickness, your wife may not be able to cook your favorite meals for a while. This will pass. Be patient, and order takeout for a few weeks. Or research a few recipes and try your hand in the kitchen!

By the seventh and eighth week of pregnancy, the baby (called a *fetus* at this point) is undergoing amazing changes. Every vital organ has started developing, and by week nine the fetus is the size of a grape. This is when you should schedule your first prenatal appointment, if you haven't had one already.

I don't want to scare you, but the first trimester is when your baby is at the most risk of suffering damage from birth defects. Certain medications, illegal drug use, alcohol consumption, and smoking can all cause birth defects. If your wife engages in any of these activities, now is the time to quit. The damage can be permanent. If your wife is having trouble quitting, think of ways you can help her quit. For example, maybe the two of you often enjoy a drink together—but making her watch you drink while she stays sober for the baby won't make it easier for her. Consider abstaining from alcohol together. Remember, you're a team, and you have to help your partner when she needs it.

Baby's Development in the First Trimester

At the end of the first trimester, the baby (about the size of a lime) has eyelids, ears, nails, genitals, and tooth buds, and can make a fist. The *placenta*, an organ that attaches to the inside of the uterus, produces hormones and transfers nutrients to the fetus via the *umbilical cord*. The umbilical cord is a group of three blood vessels: two carry blood and waste to the placenta, and one carries blood and nutrients back to the fetus. Quite literally, the umbilical cord is the baby's lifeline.

In the placenta, nutrients from the mother's blood are transferred to the fetal blood. Waste products from the fetus are transferred to the maternal blood from the fetal blood. Amazingly, this is all accomplished without the blood of the mother and the fetus mixing. Think of the placenta and umbilical cord as a natural transfer and refueling station. Even if you can't feel any movement yet, that tiny life is becoming more active every day.

Your Wife's Bodily Changes in the First Trimester

Your wife's lower abdomen may appear somewhat swollen. Her skin may also change colors in the areas around the *areola* (the darker, circular area surrounding the nipple) and on her face and neck. Dark patches on her face are commonly called the *mask of pregnancy* (*chloasma*) but normally disappear or lighten after delivery. She may have difficulty doing the same activities she enjoyed a week earlier and may become tired easily. Don't be surprised if your wife is gassier than usual too. It's all part of the baby-making process.

Gentle foot and back massages go a long way to easing discomfort at the end of the first trimester. While rubbing your wife's hands, think of your baby's tiny fists—he or she has a unique set of fingerprints now.

In addition, the first trimester brings heartburn and headaches. Kirsten suffered terrible migraines during her pregnancies, to the point where all she could do was lie down in a dark room. I spent many evenings doing dinner and bedtime duty while she rested. Be ready to step in and help out in ways you may not have before.

When to Call the Doctor

Certain symptoms may indicate more serious medical issues. Call the doctor or take your wife to the emergency room right away if she notices any of the following—they could be signs of a miscarriage or infection:

- Heavy vaginal bleeding
- Sudden, intense thirst
- Painful urination

- Fever of 101.5 degrees or greater
- Intense abdominal pain
- Sudden, severe swelling in hands, face, or legs

First Visit to the OB/GYN

The first visit to the *obstetrician/gynecologist* (OB/GYN) should be within the first four to eight weeks of pregnancy. This doctor specializes in women's reproductive health and pregnancy management.

The doctor will want to know all the details of your wife's health history, including any medical conditions or prior pregnancies. Before your visit, make a list of all the medicines that your wife takes, including vitamins. The OB/GYN will want to know of any illnesses that run in the family as well, such as diabetes or high blood pressure. Write down any questions you may have—chances are high that you'll forget about them if you don't. Once in the doctor's office, your wife will have a full checkup, including blood and urine testing, pelvic exam, weigh-in, and breast exam. You may have blood drawn as well, which will be tested for blood type and other genetic markers to determine if your baby may be prone to any abnormalities.

Our first OB/GYN appointment was at Brigham and Women's Hospital in Boston. I was nervous and excited at the same time. We parked on the street by a local sandwich shop and walked around the corner to the hospital. The one thing I was looking forward to was hearing our baby's heartbeat. I wanted to rush through the protocol of answering questions and filling out medical forms so that we could get to the main event. Finally, after what sounded like an old AM radio searching through static to find a strong signal transmission, Kirsten and I heard the muffled yet rapid *thump, thump, thump, thump* of the heartbeat. Smiles spread all around.

Second Trimester: Weeks 13–26

Think of the second trimester as the regular season in the NFL. Mother and child continue to grow in this phase of pregnancy. Stretch marks, swollen abdomen, and food cravings all make their presence known, while morning sickness tends to disappear. Women may seesaw between feeling stressed and elated; mood swings are common at this point. This is a great time to break out those love languages we discussed earlier.

Your wife may notice other physical changes in the second trimester, including the following:

- Moles may appear. If they are oddly shaped or strangely colored, call your physician.
- A dark line may form, running vertically along the midline of the abdomen. This is called *linea nigra*. This usually disappears after delivery.
- Her abdomen may be more noticeable now.
- Her legs may cramp, caused by a shortage of calcium and magnesium.
- Her body is pumping extra blood now, causing lower blood pressure and possibly dizziness. Make sure she slows down.
- She may have *varicose veins* or *hemorrhoids*—swollen blood vessels due to extra blood produced by the body.

Again, these usually shrink or disappear after delivery. Comfortable clothes, moderate exercise, and daily multivitamins can help minimize varicose veins.

- Most healthy women gain around five to ten pounds by the start of the second trimester. Your wife may not look like she's pregnant, but she definitely looks different than she did three months ago.
- Her skin may break out as if she were a teenager again.
- She may have groin pain, caused by the softening of the hip joints to make room for the baby. Kirsten suffered to the point that rolling out of bed was difficult. *Diastasis symphysis pubis* is when the joints widen too far. If this happens, the OB/GYN may prescribe certain exercises or recommend wearing a pelvic support belt if the pain is too intense.

During the second trimester of her third pregnancy, much of Kirsten's morning sickness had subsided, but she faced a new set of challenges. Her abdomen had expanded, putting pressure on her lower back. This meant ongoing backaches and terrible groin pain. She slept with a pillow between her legs (some women purchase a full-body pillow), did gentle stretches every morning, and occasionally sat on a birthing ball, which helped take the weight of the baby off her pelvis for a while. Since I have some knowledge of the body's compensation patterns, I occasionally massaged her lower back, glutes, and hips to take the pressure off the adductors. The pain eventually went away after she delivered the baby.

The fetus is undergoing massive development in the second trimester. An *ultrasound* (an exam that uses sound waves to generate pictures of the fetus) can detect the baby's sex at about twenty weeks. The baby has a full skeleton and is moving around in the womb. You may even feel the baby kick at this point! He or she is looking a lot like a newborn too, putting on necessary fat and growing hair.

Your Role during the Second Trimester Is Greater Than You Think

You may play a surprisingly large role in keeping your wife healthy during the second trimester. Women are more likely to suffer from urinary tract infections (UTIs) during this time than earlier in the pregnancy because the uterus is growing and is on top of the bladder. Pressure from the uterus can prevent the bladder from draining. Urine remaining in the bladder can become infected with bacteria. Sexual intercourse can increase the chances of your wife getting a UTI. This doesn't mean that sex is out of the picture until after delivery, but there are some precautions you and your wife can take to reduce the likelihood of an infection occurring. Encourage your wife to do the following:

- Hydrate. Drink at least six to eight glasses of water daily. Cranberry juice is a natural diuretic.
- Urinate before and after sex.
- Wear cotton underwear.

A UTI can be treated with antibiotics. But don't ignore it. UTIs can lead to kidney infections, and these simple steps will go a long way to avoiding them.

Keeping the Right Attitude

Don't think "she owes me" when you're helping out and keeping your wife comfortable. Really, you owe her more than she owes you. She is carrying your child. It's a tough job, and I hope that by understanding the science behind pregnancy you'll have a better appreciation and awareness of how complex this process is.

I have worked with men who think pregnancy is an excuse for a woman to sit around the house eating candy, and a time to get extra work out of her husband. Sure, there are a few women out there who do that, but I have a feeling that the majority of women are doing everything except taking it easy during pregnancy, especially if they have children already or careers outside the home. Have you ever tried taking care of a full house of children under the age of ten? Try it for thirty minutes, then see if you have time to put your feet up. Now imagine doing that while pregnant. I think you'll come out of the experience with a different attitude.

I've heard men chatter in the locker room about their jobs, complaining about how hard they work and how little their wives do. "I work hard all day! What's my wife doing at home?" they grouse.

Whether you're in the NFL or selling insurance, your job is difficult, but try to remember that your wife is working too, even if she's at home caring for the family. In my humble opinion, being a mom, especially one who stays at home 24/7, is the most challenging job known to humankind. And if she has a career outside the home, she has an entirely different set of responsibilities. Do you ever help out around the house? Or, as you both walk through the door after a long day at work, do you head for the couch when she heads to the kitchen to prepare dinner? If she's pregnant, that's another job to add to her list. Think about that. As I've said before, pull your weight. You're a team.

Other Considerations during the Second Trimester

Have you made a birth plan yet? We talked about this in chapter 2. If not, the second trimester is the time to do it. The third trimester goes by in a flash, and you don't want to be caught with your guard down. Start preparing the nursery—set up the crib and stroller, get the car seat ready to install, and prewash the baby's clothes. Consider baby-proofing the house before the baby becomes mobile. Enroll in an infant CPR and first aid class as well. They're usually offered at local community centers, or your physician may be able to recommend classes.

The Playoffs, aka the Third Trimester, Weeks 27–40

We've made it into the most exciting part of the pregnancy. There's no mistaking it now: a baby is on the way! Your wife's abdomen has probably grown to the size of a soccer ball, and the baby weighs about two pounds. Don't worry, the baby will put on weight quickly as the third trimester progresses, ultimately weighing anywhere from six to ten pounds.

By the twenty-eighth week, your wife will have more frequent prenatal visits to the OB/GYN—probably every week until she delivers. You may hear some of the following terms during these appointments:

- *Rh factor.* We all have one of four blood types: A, AB, B, or O. The Rh factor is a protein that sits on red blood cells. Those with the Rh protein on their red blood cells are *Rh-positive*, those without it are *Rh-negative*. When you and your wife find out your blood types (during one of her first prenatal visits), she will also learn her Rh factor. Being Rh-positive is common—more than 85 percent of the population is, and it doesn't impact general health. Problems occur during pregnancy when the mother's blood doesn't have the Rh factor (i.e., when the mother is Rh-negative) and the baby's blood does. Half of all children born to an Rh-negative mother and an Rh-positive father will be Rh-positive. During pregnancy, there's a chance that the mother's blood and the baby's blood could mix. If that happens, the mother's blood may treat the baby's blood like an allergen or infection and try to destroy the fetus. Untreated, this can lead to miscarriages or *ectopic pregnancies* (pregnancies that occur outside the uterus). If your wife is Rh-negative, she may receive an injection of *RhoGAM*, a vaccine-like substance that can prevent blood problems from occurring.

- *Fetal movement chart*. This is also known as *kick counts*. The American Congress of Obstetricians and Gynecologists recommends timing how long it takes to feel ten kicks.[1] Anything within two hours is ideal. As your wife gets closer to delivery day, chances are she'll feel more than ten kicks in that time. Kicking, fluttering, and rolling are signs of a healthy baby.
- *Natural childbirth*. This refers to having a baby with little to no medical intervention. Breathing techniques (such as Lamaze or the Alexander technique) are helpful in pushing through the pain. Consider attending a

childbirth class that explains proper breathing techniques if your wife is pursuing a natural delivery. After a successful epidural with our first child and an unsuccessful one with our second, Kirsten elected to "go natural" with her last three deliveries. There are pros and cons to each, mainly pertaining to recovery time for the mother, length of labor, and some effects on the baby. There are many options when it comes to delivering a baby, including water birth and even home birth. We have done all of the above! Explore these options with your wife and your doctor, and decide what is best for your family.

- *Caesarean section.* Also called a *C-section*, this is when a mother's abdomen is cut and the baby is surgically removed from the womb.

- *Episiotomy.* This is a surgical incision that is made during labor to enlarge the vaginal opening. This procedure is not performed as frequently today as in the past, but it is still employed if there isn't enough room for the baby, if the baby is showing signs of distress, or if the mother cannot control her ability to push. Make sure that you discuss this with your wife's doctor, and if you do not want this procedure performed, state clearly that this procedure is only to be performed as a last resort. (We had a doctor who was all too eager to perform the procedure upon entering the birthing room. With loud voices, we let her know not to proceed!)

Your Wife's Body

Besides the changes on the outside, your wife's body has undergone miraculous changes on the inside as well. Some pregnancy symptoms from the first trimester (fatigue, mood swings) may reappear during the third trimester. Other changes to look for include the following:

- Insomnia. Your wife may have difficulty finding a comfortable sleeping position and difficulty sleeping as a result. In addition, she may be more tired now than she was earlier in her pregnancy. If her insomnia worsens, consult her physician.

- Foot growth. There are so many hormones being produced that they can cause joints to loosen. Remember Kirsten's groin pain? That was caused by her hip joints loosening. Extra hormones can also cause feet to grow— some women's feet may go up an entire shoe size. If this happens, it is permanent, but console your wife with the idea that now she has a perfect excuse to buy new shoes.

- Breast discharge. A yellowish, creamy substance called *colostrum* may begin to leak from her breasts. It is also known as premilk, and is thicker than regular milk. Not all women leak colostrum, though it is normal.

- Braxton Hicks contractions. These are also called "practice contractions." A *contraction* is when the muscles of the uterus tighten—usually for thirty to sixty seconds. Braxton Hicks contractions don't actually lead to labor and delivery. Some women notice them more than others.

- Heartburn and inability to eat normal portions without feeling nauseous.

After the thirty-eighth week of pregnancy, the baby is continuing to grow, but most organs are fully functioning.

The cervix will *efface*, or soften, as delivery day approaches. When the cervix is completely effaced, expect labor to happen soon.

Having Faith in the Miracle of Life

As a father, I know this is a lot to take in. But I hope you'll take a step back and recognize the miracle of development going on. I remember the first ultrasound, where the doctor pointed to Grace's head and spine, and I heard her heartbeat. I was overwhelmed. During a 4-D ultrasound, which I highly recommend, I watched Grace yawn in utero. Yawns are contagious, even from the womb—I yawned, then Kirsten yawned. We were all connected in that moment, and in that moment I forgot my fears, my anxiety, and my never-ending baby-preparation list. Though the X's and O's of pregnancy are important to know, a family needs love and strength to persevere.

Strength through the Lord

Are you overwhelmed, wondering how you're going to make it to week forty? You will bond with your wife as your baby develops, even if you're totally out of your comfort zone. Kirsten and I found strength in the Lord and trusted that he would guide us through. Our faith kept us strong, through the difficult times and the joyous ones, and it continues to light the way for my family. At times I felt inadequate. Truth be told, I still do. Sometimes, I don't see myself as wise enough, strong enough, faithful enough, or patient enough to be someone's daddy and someone's husband. I cannot be

X's and O's

the father and husband my family needs me to be with my strength alone. Only through the power of the Lord can I lead them as I should, knowing that when I fall short, he is always there. His strength is made perfect in my weakness.

These can be frightening times. With each pregnancy, we have worried about the health of our growing baby. So much can go wrong, and each visit with a healthy report is a blessing. Between the internet, friends, and family, every worst-case scenario may be discussed. Though I wish we had done it more, Kirsten and I spent time praying together, not only for her health, but for the health of our babies. We also prayed that if a problem arose, we would have the strength, wisdom, and unity to confront it. Even if this is not your first child, the uncertainty of pregnancy drives us to rely on God.

I hope this chapter empowers you to be part of the process and to feel more actively involved. Your family will benefit from your participation and your leadership.

CHAPTER SIX

Bed Check

Her Body Is Changing and So Are Her Needs

Now that we've covered the biology of pregnancy, I'd like to talk about what to expect in terms of how you can make your wife feel like a queen. Perhaps now more than ever before in your relationship, your wife will look to you for comfort and assurance that all the changes she is undergoing—weight gain, acne, morning sickness—will not change your love for her. I'll also talk about maternity clothes, photo shoots, and your role of keeping the family together.

From Small to XXL: Make Her Feel Sexy as She Grows

In 2008, when Kirsten was pregnant with our first daughter, Grace, she had a hard time finding maternity clothes that were trendy and comfortable. I wanted her to feel as radiant as she looked. I remember sitting in the New England Patriots locker room after practice one day, looking up stylish maternity clothing on the internet. Up popped a company called Isabella Oliver, a London-based fashion house that only makes luxurious, wearable maternity outfits.

This particular brand is rather expensive, with prices ranging from fifty to three hundred dollars per piece, but I liked their story—clothing for women to make them feel like themselves during pregnancy. So there I sat on the locker room floor, speaking with a customer service representative in England and ordering clothes for Kirsten. I was so excited to find a way to make Kirsten feel beautiful that I went a little overboard and ordered an entire wardrobe. I kept it a surprise, and when the package arrived, she was thrilled that I had thought about her and taken this step to help her feel like her pre-pregnancy self.

Am I saying you should blow your budget on expensive maternity wear? Not at all. This was just one way to show Kirsten that I was paying attention. I wanted her to feel good, and that meant finding fashionable clothes that fit. What does this mean for you?

First, do a little research. Ask your wife what might make her happy. Then, keeping your budget in mind, find something that will increase her sense of well-being. If your wife dislikes the idea of abandoning her trendy outfits for nine months, but high-end maternity clothes aren't in the cards, there are plenty of companies—Pea in the Pod, Destination Maternity, and H&M Maternity are great examples—that sell the latest trends in chic maternity wear but won't break the bank.

A Maternity Photo Shoot Surprise

Kirsten and I had four more children after Grace, and each pregnancy was different, from the severity of her migraines to the intensity of her morning sickness. During her fourth pregnancy, I set up a surprise maternity photo shoot for Kirsten. I thought it would be a fun way to boost her self-confidence and have a few hours just to herself without worrying about her day-to-day responsibilities.

It's very different taking care of a growing family while pregnant—any pampering and downtime she enjoyed during the first pregnancy went right out the window with the subsequent babies—and I wanted her to have a few visual memories of this special time. Keeping the photo shoot a surprise required a little more planning than just ordering some outfits online, so I enlisted help.

At the time, I was playing for the Browns and we were living in Cleveland. We planned to take our three children to Disney World for a few days in March to get away from the cold weather. To get the photo shoot just right, I called one of Kirsten's friends, a model living in Tampa. I figured she might know her way around a photo shoot and asked if she would arrange one for my wife. I wanted Kirsten to sit for a high-fashion maternity session, kind of like the glossy spreads you see in magazines. Kirsten's friend was all over it. She guided me on what kind of outfits to buy, and to maintain the element of surprise, I shipped everything to her house.

The friend contacted a photographer, makeup artist, and hairstylist, and booked a session at a nearby studio. My job was the most challenging: getting Kirsten from Orlando to Tampa without blowing the surprise. To be honest, I don't remember what I told her, but somehow I convinced her to leave Disney, pack everyone in the car, and drive ninety minutes to Tampa.

As we approached a nondescript building in the middle of the city, I could tell that Kirsten had no idea what was going on. I told her about the photo shoot once I stopped the car, and that this was her time to relax and enjoy some time alone. While the kids and I went to a nearby Cracker Barrel, she spent three hours being pampered with full makeup, hairstyling, and beautiful clothes. That afternoon was all about her. It wasn't about anybody else. It wasn't about the kids or me. It was just about her being and feeling beautiful. I look at those photos every once in a while, and they make me smile because I remember how happy she was that day.

You can find a way to make your wife feel special too. And you should put some thought into it. She's going through a lot of changes now, and if you're willing to put in a little effort, and get a few friends to help out, you could put together an exciting event that celebrates the creation of life and the woman who's doing the lion's share of the work. Being pregnant is hard, and by taking the time to make your wife feel special, you're also making those forty weeks more bearable.

You can still create a special moment for your spouse even if your budget and time frame are modest. Below are a few suggestions of ways to show your wife you love and appreciate her:

- *Maternity photo shoot.* These aren't as exclusive as they were six years ago, and the price points range dramatically. Now boutique portrait galleries and big-box stores like Target offer maternity photography sessions, and Pinterest has thousands of links explaining how to create a picture-perfect belly shoot. Or you can take the pictures yourself if you're comfortable with a camera. Either way, make the whole day about her.

- *Prenatal massage.* Book a series of prenatal massages. If you have older children, make the appointment on the weekend, and you keep the kids engaged for the day. These targeted massages can go a long way to relieving back pain, improving sleep, and boosting morale.

- *The gift of sleep.* This is one of the easiest and most affordable presents you can give your wife. She needs to sleep now as much as possible—hormonal changes, restless leg syndrome, sleep apnea, and nighttime urination make getting a solid eight hours of shut-eye during pregnancy challenging. Nursing and caring for a newborn mean sleepless nights are ahead as well. If you have older children, take them out for the day and let your wife hit the snooze button for as long as she wants. Consider leaving a flower and a note at her bedside, wishing her sweet dreams.

- *Pregnancy gift basket.* These can be a thoughtful way of helping your wife deal with bodily changes like stretch marks and ashy skin. Take away the guesswork by looking for prepackaged gift baskets with unscented body lotion, cocoa butter, lip balm, and other products specifically for pregnant women.

- *Keepsake journal.* Whether it's a specific pregnancy journal complete with writing prompts and fill-in-the-blanks, a week-to-week format, or a simple, leather-bound volume, give your wife a private place to record her thoughts and emotions. Select a journal that's lightweight and easy to carry, so whether the urge to write strikes at 3:00 a.m. or at work, your wife can jot down whatever she's feeling and thinking before she gets a case of "baby brain" and forgets.

• *Body pillows.* Kirsten suffered from intense hip and back pain, and although we looked into purchasing a body pillow, we never did. Instead, she just used extra pillows between the knees and a few more as pelvis support. Body pillows are a great invention, though. They look like a number 9 and are shaped to contour to a woman's body as it grows throughout pregnancy. These pillows provide belly and neck support while your wife is sleeping and will subsequently improve overall quality of sleep during this tough time. Body pillows generally cost about fifty dollars, and, as mentioned above, the gift of a good night's sleep is priceless.

Push Presents: To Give or Not to Give?

Never heard of a push present? You're not alone. It's a gift that mothers sometimes receive from their husbands after giving birth. When some husbands want to acknowledge the hard work of having a baby, they buy their wives "push presents." And, mostly thanks to celebrity couples like Kim Kardashian and Kanye West, these presents have become stratospheric in cost. (After Kardashian gave birth to her second child, West presented her with a diamond-studded choker valued in the millions of dollars.)

While celebrating the birth of a child with a gift isn't new, many men are feeling increased pressure to buy expensive gifts like jewelry and even lavish trips to outdo their friends. There is no standard on whether to give a push present or not, and feel free to avoid peer pressure from co-workers or friends. This is an intimate time, and it's your call whether you want to participate in this trend or not. More often than not, your wife would prefer a simple gesture of love rather than an extravagant gift bought in the heat of the moment.

Creating Special Moments Every Day: Rest Is Best

Just before Eden was born, I was looking for another way to create a special moment for Kirsten. We had already done the surprise maternity fashion shoot, enjoyed a last-minute babymoon in Times Square, and by that time, I ran out of ideas. Then it hit me: Kirsten is with the kids all day every day. When she's pregnant, she often suffers from terrible migraines, but that doesn't mean she gets to call in a sick day. What she wanted more than anything was a day of total rest.

I booked a night for her at a local hotel, and I stayed home with the kids. It wasn't fancy or far away, but it was just distant enough that she couldn't come home if something came up. She had an evening and morning to herself. (Hello, room service!) When you already have children, the hardest thing for a mother to do is to find time for herself, especially when she is pregnant. Moms are accustomed to putting everyone else's needs above their own, even during pregnancy when they should be resting as much as possible.

No matter how much progress has been made in terms of equal partnership and child-raising, I still think fathers have it easier. When the going gets tough at home, we can slip away to work, where we can hide behind our desks (or helmets) for a few hours. Many women don't often have that same break, especially if they are at home full-time with young children. I also think that women who have careers outside the home end up doing the lion's share of child-raising. Kirsten worked all the way up until our first daughter was born, and her bouts with migraines and morning sickness made that difficult. Since then, she's made the decision to be home with our children, homeschooling the oldest two, and it's still a challenge for her to find five minutes of quiet and solitude.

If a weekend away isn't possible, try corralling the kids on Saturday morning and letting your wife enjoy the downtime. During the week, consider putting the kids to bed so she doesn't have to. Sometimes, just by listening, you're creating a special, intimate moment when she can vent, chat, or simply tell you how her day went. That's a great gift too.

Travel and Loneliness: A Cautionary Tale

Believe it or not, I don't travel that much for my job. We do have away games, but out of a sixteen-game season, we only travel for eight of them. Generally, I'm away for two days at a time. However, in 2008 I experienced an unusual travel schedule. I was still with New England then, and we had back-to-back games on the West Coast. First we played in Seattle, and then stayed on the West Coast to play Oakland the following Sunday. I ended up spending ten days away from home.

While we were playing in Seattle, I scored a touchdown. At that moment, I realized that Kirsten was back home in Boston, nine months pregnant and watching me on television. In the end zone, I put the football under my jersey and rubbed it like I was pregnant. I pointed at the camera too. Basically, that was my way of saying, "Babe, I know you're home watching, I know you're pregnant, and I love you." It was my way of celebrating. It was innocent enough, but the NFL has a rule against using the football as a prop. The referees threw a flag and there was a fifteen-yard penalty. You can imagine how Belichick felt about that!

Later that week, after I had returned home, I received a FedEx envelope. In the NFL, whenever you get a little FedEx envelope, you know you've been fined. And sure enough, I was fined—$10,000.

I've never done that again. I love my wife, but that was an expensive display of affection! Happily, after I explained my motives to the NFL appeals officer, the fine was reduced to $5,000 because I wasn't taunting Seattle; I was paying tribute to my wife and my first child. Though we don't have a lot of football memorabilia in the house, we framed a news article about the event. It's in Grace's room, and one day it will make a great show-and-tell prop.

Now, I just call Kirsten when I want to check in. The point of all this is that whether you travel as a professional athlete or a corporate warrior, it can be difficult to find ways to be present. Call, text, send flowers, or set up dinner for her; they're all long-distance ways of being part of the pregnancy process when you're far from home. Just don't put a football under your jersey on national television after scoring a touchdown.

Raising Kids and Being Perfect Are Incompatible

Many parents, Kirsten and I included, are often prepared to renounce all their personal pleasures and interests and totally devote themselves to child-rearing. Some folks call that perfectionism, and nobody's more of a perfectionist than me. I've been this way since childhood. For years I accepted nothing less than perfect in my efforts on the field and in my personal life. It was a difficult line to toe. I like to look at cooking as an example of how my perfectionist tendencies used to get in the way of my willingness to try something new. Early in our marriage, I hated to cook because I felt that anything less than perfect was unacceptable, and I'm not a perfect cook. So I wouldn't even attempt putting a pot on the stove to boil, let alone making a meal.

As my family has grown, I've realized that I'm not going to be perfect, and that's all right. I've realized that I might mess up, but I might make something great too. At home or on the gridiron, practice makes progress, if not perfection. In short, I've realized I need to offer myself and others the same grace God gives us: merit not based on my performance but on the work of his Son. This is the source from which we parent and love well.

Now I'm willing to try things (like cooking) with the understanding that the end result may not be what I was originally hoping for, but I'll never improve if I don't try. And if I turn a hamburger into a moon rock my self-worth hasn't changed a bit. (Yes, I did char a burger the first time I tried to grill.) That mentality applies to parenting as well. Children are not perfect, and we cannot expect that our children will do exactly as we command. More likely than not, they will wake up in the middle of the night, they will disobey, and their interests and temperaments may be vastly different from yours. Pressure to be perfect doesn't produce perfect children. Acceptance, love, and a willingness to learn from our spouses and our children are the ingredients for a happy and healthy family.

If you're a perfectionist, you may find pregnancy incredibly difficult. You may wonder why your wife isn't able to participate in the same activities as before, and you may expect that nothing will (or should) change in your relationship or your share of household chores until the baby arrives. Many women juggle multiple responsibilities in the home and in their careers, and need assistance. From a physical standpoint, there are some activities that women shouldn't be doing when they're pregnant anyway, like picking up cat litter and lifting heavy objects. You need to help out. Your wife isn't expecting perfection from you—she's expecting a helping hand.

Let's reverse the scenario for a minute. Would I expect Kirsten to perform my job exactly the way I do? Hardly. But if I needed help and she could provide it, I would gratefully accept it and lay my perfectionist expectations aside.

As the pregnancy progresses, your wife's ability to cope with day-to-day activities will change. For example, I remember driving down Commonwealth Avenue in Boston with Kirsten, and she was still in her first trimester with Grace. All of a sudden, morning sickness got the best of her. She had to pull over so she could vomit. I sat in amazement as she resumed driving like nothing had happened! The strength of a woman! It was unpleasant, to say the least, but I bore no judgment, nor did I expect her to perk up and feel better. In addition, she was also still working outside the home, and every night she came home totally exhausted. I saw that and realized that I had to pitch in around the house if we were going to be a true team.

Don't Be a Jerk: Get Out of Your Comfort Zone

For you men out there who think, *I'm not going to cook or clean. That's women's work*, I would say: welcome to the 2000s. But it's not even about the year, it's about a man doing his job. Don't be a jerk. Get over yourself. Grab a sponge and roll up your sleeves. As I've outlined above, and I'll repeat here, there will be things you have to do to keep your relationship strong through the pregnancy. There will be times when you'll look at your wife and wonder how she's doing so much, and other times when she won't be able to lift her head off the pillow.

Some women will keep pushing through the pain and the discomfort in order to meet their responsibilities, whether they're work related or personal. I think women are used to putting up with discomfort more than men are, so when your wife looks to you for help, she must be feeling really miserable. You will have to help out more around the house than you may like. Once the baby arrives, you're in this together, and your responsibilities will grow with your child. Be ready for it.

I mentioned cooking and perfectionism before. I'm bringing up cooking again because it was something that I had never really done before Kirsten was pregnant. I've always helped out with washing dishes, bedtime, cleaning the house, and picking up the slack when Kirsten didn't feel well. But cooking was new for me. There were three weeks during the last pregnancy when Kirsten suffered horrible migraines and I became Mr. Mom. In addition to bedtime, bath time, and playtime, I shopped for groceries after everyone went to bed and prepared them for the next day. I cooked too. Were my meals gourmet feasts? Not at all. But I was willing to do whatever it took to keep the family functioning.

What's the point here? Take care of your wife like you'd want to be taken care of. Treat your wife as you would treat your body. (Because according to God's Word, she is part of your body!) Granted, most men have no idea how they would want to be treated during pregnancy, but imagine how you would feel if your body and emotions changed daily and you had very little control over the process. Keep that in mind. Be willing to go out of your comfort zone and pitch in. I may sound like a broken record by now, but communication is critical here. Ask her what she needs, and provide that assistance.

I've reached the point that I can tell just by looking at Kirsten whether she's feeling all right or not. If she doesn't look like she can handle cooking odors, I'll surf the web for a simple recipe, make my way to the kitchen, and tie on an apron. I still may not be a great cook, but if I have well-written directions, I can execute a meal.

You can't use the excuse that you can't cook or clean or change diapers because you didn't grow up doing those things. Plenty of women didn't grow up cleaning or cooking either, yet many men are still hardwired to expect women to automatically take on these domestic activities. It's not fair. While these activities won't feel natural to you, you've got to give it a shot for the good of the team.

The pregnancy process is about growth. There's physical growth—your wife's bodily changes—interpersonal growth, and emotional and spiritual growth. Being willing to step up and be an equal partner in the pregnancy process is daunting, but it's for the good of the whole family. You may even surprise yourself and find that you enjoy these new responsibilities. I still don't love cooking, but I am comfortable with my ability to play second string when my first-string teammate is out. And I get great satisfaction when my kids say, "This is good, Daddy!"

Final Thoughts: Hang in There

This is a lot to take in: your wife's physical and emotional changes as well as your own emotions, potential sibling rivalry, and maintaining an open and honest relationship. Pregnancy is a marathon with obstacles. If you stay on track, you will finish this race. There are hundreds of moving parts between conception and delivery, and you will see success if you are willing to adapt. I've found that the way to get through the tough times is to have a goal. If you have no desire to make your relationship work, then when the going gets tough, you'll bail.

Too many men can't set their sights on the endgame. Don't be like the average man. Don't be that guy who gives up when he encounters a setback in his marriage or with his children. Be different, because I know you can be. That's why I wrote this book: to remind you that being a positive role model in the life of your wife and children is possible, even when you think it isn't. Sometimes it takes one man to confide in another for change to happen—guy talk. If you aren't perfect (and remember, no parent is), don't give up. Stay the course. Your family is worth your commitment.

CHAPTER SEVEN

Baby Showers

They're Not Just for Women Anymore

As the oldest of six children, I helped my parents a lot when it came to raising my siblings. I changed diapers, played peekaboo, and read books to my younger brothers and sisters, but helping out didn't mean I was granted access to baby showers. My mother and her circle of friends often hosted baby showers when one of them became pregnant, and they were strictly women only. I remember my mother telling my father that she would be attending a baby shower, and there was no question that this party was for the ladies.

In my preadolescent brain, I thought baby showers were literal events, where the mother-to-be took a shower and rubbed her belly or held her newborn baby while the other ladies gathered around and watched. Kids think the craziest things, but besides the misunderstanding, I remember feeling left out. I enjoyed caring for my younger siblings, and I would have liked to see what really went on at a baby shower, because even if it wasn't what I imagined in my head, I understood that a baby shower was a celebration of a new life.

Even when Kirsten and I started having children, our first baby shower was for women only. NFL linebacker Rosevelt Colvin is a buddy of mine, and we were both playing for New England in 2008 when Kirsten was pregnant with Grace. Colvin's wife, Tiffany, planned and hosted that baby shower. Many of the Patriots' wives and girlfriends were there, and Kirsten told me she had a wonderful time, which is the most important thing to remember, but, just like when I was a child, I still felt sidelined. By the time we were in Cleveland, Kirsten was pregnant with Isaiah, and we had developed a solid community of friends and colleagues.

One evening Kirsten asked me how I felt about a coed baby shower, and of course I was all in. My teammate Reggie Hodges and his wife Arin hosted the party, and Arin, along with Kirsten, planned the whole thing. It was a coed affair from the get-go, so the guys knew there would be other teammates even before they arrived at the house. Ten couples—mostly NFL players and their spouses—helped celebrate Isaiah's approaching arrival, and I finally got to see what happened at a baby shower. Guess what—we had a blast, and everyone there had the opportunity to share our love for Kirsten and Isaiah.

I know what you're thinking, but please, don't put down this book! This isn't 1966 anymore. Men are in the delivery room, and they're part of the baby celebration parties too. I hope I can change your mind with this chapter if you're feeling squeamish or still think that baby showers should remain just for women. In the following pages, I'll talk about the evolution of this trend, and even though you may feel indifferent or even totally opposed right now, perhaps you'll have a change of heart by the time I'm through. It's always nice to be included, especially for family occasions. You may be surprised to learn that you actually can enjoy these parties—it sure surprised me.

Imagine a group of NFL linebackers, punters, wide receivers, and quarterbacks. Think Seneca Wallace, Joe Thomas, and others, all teammates, huddled in my living room, smelling chocolate-laced diapers, trying to detect the candy bar flavor melted inside. Sound outrageous? It happened at Kirsten's baby shower in Cleveland. If that scenario sounds unlikely to you, you're not alone. Parents whose children were born fifteen or twenty years ago may read this and scratch their heads—what are men doing at a baby shower? Times change, and the stigma of men being involved in traditionally women-centered events is fading, even for tough NFL players. If my friends from the NFL can get over their predispositions, so can you.

The Evolution of the Coed Baby Shower: A Brief History

Historically, baby showers were women-only affairs, as I briefly discussed above, and men didn't feel left out in the slightest. With the women safely out of sight for a few hours, men were free to indulge in binge-watching sports and kicking back on the sofa. These guys weren't unhappy. They were fine with spending quality time with their televisions.

But men have become more involved in parenting in the past two decades, and that means taking part in celebrating the happy arrival. Where the traditional baby shower included cake, gifts, and silly games, the coed baby shower (also known as a "Jack and Jill" baby shower) incorporates those elements with a slightly more masculine twist. At Kirsten's baby shower for Isaiah, rather than frilly frosted cupcakes, our menu was simple: hearty sandwiches and soda. We played party games and guessed baby food based on smell. Kirsten and I opened presents, and overall, it was a nice reason to get all of our friends together and enjoy one another's company. While we kept our party low-key, I've read about elaborate coed baby showers that include travel and plenty of adult beverages.

This is a new trend, and you may be saying, "Benjamin, do I really have to do this? It just feels so unmanly." If you and your wife are hosting a couples' event, you will not be the only man there, so right away that should ease some nerves. Our coed baby shower seemed more like a big party with friends that we loved and could lean on for support and guidance. At first some of my teammates did not want to come. "I'll be the only guy there!" they told me. But when these guys saw that it was a couples' party, they showed up. If you're facing the same kind of heat from your buddies, stand tall and stick to your guns. Your friends will come around. Feeling braver? Below are a few suggestions on how you and your wife can throw a fun coed baby shower that won't send your male buddies running for the locker room:

- *Talk to your wife first.* Make sure your wife actually wants to have a coed baby shower. Some women may view this as a time to bond with their female friends, and if that's what she wants, you have to respect her wishes. If she doesn't give you the go-ahead, you can still plan a "man shower," which I'll talk about later in this chapter. If she wants a traditional baby shower, consider showing up to her shower at the very end, just after the presents have been opened and guests are about to leave. Bring a beautiful bouquet of flowers, and I have a feeling she'll be thrilled with the surprise. If she's on board for a couples' party, read on. *Note:* Some women won't want a shower of any kind, due to religious beliefs or other concerns. Make sure you're aware of this before proceeding.

- *Pick a theme.* Since this is a coed party, you probably won't want to festoon your space with pink decorations. Keep the colors gender neutral (unless you want to highlight the baby's gender) and the décor casual. Consider incorporating a theme that will keep the men and the women happy—sports teams are good places to look for inspiration. My teammates from Cleveland came to our shower, so we had a major Browns theme throughout, and it didn't hurt that the shower was for a boy. Invite your friends to come wearing their favorite team's jersey.

- *Have lots of simple food.* A baby shower isn't the appropriate venue for hiring a three-piece band, and traditionally, the food has been the focal point. Food is still important in the coed version, but you'll have to change your game plan if you're inviting men. First of all, you'll need much more food than you would if the event were just for women—men don't like finger food for lunch, and NFL players have hearty appetites! You shouldn't be slaving over a barbecue either. Think about what men eat when they're all watching Sunday football: chicken wings, chips, pizza, mixed nuts, and deli sandwiches. If that menu sounds too masculine, consider a make-your-own taco bar, or have the party catered. If you don't want the men dialing Domino's, make sure that whatever you serve pleases everyone.

- *Have fun with desserts.* We served Dirty Diaper Cookies, which were sugar cookies filled with melted chocolate. You can simply melt chocolate bars and call it a day, or do something a bit more complicated. I'm not a great cook, but these are easy to make and are guaranteed crowd-pleasers. Here's the recipe for ten large cookies. (Double it if you're entertaining more guests.)

———— Dirty Diaper Cookies ————

1 tube	sugar cookie dough
	flour for rolling out dough
	mini candy bars in assorted flavors
	(like Mr. Goodbar and Krackel)
½ cup	milk
3 cups	powdered sugar
4 ounces	chocolate chips
	piping bag and decorator tips
	(for diaper pins)
	ruler (like I said, I'm a perfectionist)
	scissors

1. Preheat the oven to 350 degrees.
2. Shape the dough. Use your ruler to measure and cut out a paper triangle (8½" x 7" x 7"). Flour your work surface and roll out the dough. Place the paper triangle on top of the dough and cut out as many triangles as possible. Reshape and roll the remaining dough, and repeat the process. You will fold each triangle into a diaper in step 3.

102

3. Fill and fold. Position each triangle so that you are looking at it upside down, like this:

Place an *unwrapped* candy bar in the middle of each triangle. Fold the bottom corner over the candy bar, then fold the left and right corners into the middle. Place each filled cookie on a parchment-lined baking sheet. (You can also use cooking spray or butter to grease the pan instead of parchment.)

4. Bake the cookies in the preheated oven for 12 minutes. Remove cookies from the oven. Transfer cookies to a wire rack. Let cookies cool for 30 minutes. Serve the cookies as they are, or continue with the following two steps.

5. Create diaper pins by heating chocolate chips in a microwave-safe bowl for 30 seconds. Stir and reheat until chips are melted. Here's where artistry comes in handy: print images of safety pins—yes, they're on the internet—and place the printout under a sheet of parchment paper. This will serve as your template. Assemble the piping bag with a decorator tip, and pour the melted chocolate into the bag. Pipe the chocolate over the image of the pins. The first few will be awful, but you'll get better. Allow the chocolate to harden.

6. Make the cookie glaze. Combine ½ cup milk with 3 cups powdered sugar. Pour the glaze over the cookies. It shouldn't look perfect.

7. Assemble the cookies. Remove chocolate pins from parchment paper and place on top of the glaze. The glaze will act like glue and keep the pins from moving.

- *Plan party games.* Guests expect games at baby showers. They are a great way to get people talking with one another. We played the Dirty Diaper Game, where we melted different chocolate bars and smeared them in disposable diapers. We laid the diapers on a table, and players had to smell them and write down what they thought was in each one. Some folks even opened the diapers to examine and taste the contents! Players with the most correct answers win. A similar game is Guess the Beer in the Baby Bottle, where you fill baby bottles (don't reuse these for your baby!) with different beers, and players have to guess which beer is in each bottle.

- *Provide party favors.* Bags of color-coordinated M&Ms are a neat touch. Seed packets are a nifty reminder of the new life soon to arrive.

When you plan a coed baby shower right, you'll be bringing couples together while also celebrating the new baby. You'll eat, open gifts, and laugh. Isn't that what family is all about?

Man Shower: Celebrating Dad-to-Be

This is a trend that has just emerged in the last few years. Basically, groups of men became a little jealous and felt alienated when their wives attended various baby showers and decided that they ought to have a party just for men. These guys purposefully avoided traditional baby shower games and activities and just did what made them happy. They played bingo, drank some beer, opened a few gag gifts, shared their story on social media, and a new concept was born. Some parties are more intricate than others, where hosts include competitive events like a diaper football toss and a blindfolded baby stroller relay course. It seems that mothers have been inspired to throw parties that celebrate the soon-to-be newborn while dads mellow out and indulge in a little male bonding.

I've never been to a dads-only baby shower—it's such a new concept that it didn't even exist when my last child, Eden, was born. After researching what information is available about the booming "man shower" concept, I have a few dos and don'ts on how to help you arrange a great guys' get-together without it turning into a bachelor party.

- *It's not a bachelor party.* Should I say that again? A baby shower for men is not an excuse to get blasted and hit the strip club. At its core, a baby shower is about celebrating the birth of a baby. It's certainly a milestone moment, like marriage, but this isn't just about adults. Don't use your unborn child as an excuse to drink and watch football all afternoon.

- *Invite men with children.* Guys without kids might feel incredibly out of place at a baby shower, so limit the guest list to men who already have kids or who are expecting children. This is also a great opportunity for first-time fathers to get advice from veteran dads on parenting.

- *Bring out the competitive spirit.* Plan a few games such as those mentioned above, like diaper football toss and baby stroller races. I've even read about baby betting, where guests place bets on what day they think the baby will arrive.

- *Choose a masculine theme.* That's right, no pastel pink here. Military-inspired camouflage, football gear, and martial arts are all possible, but don't feel constrained— the sky's the limit. Go online to create an awesome invitation that reflects your spirit.

- *Think of daddy-appropriate gifts.* Nowadays, every- thing from socks to diaper bags can be customized. I've seen diaper bags shaped like tool kits, T-shirts with silly phrases like, "The Man Behind the Bump," and bibs with "Oh, Spit!" written on them.

- *Overwhelmed? Enlist help.* Want to throw a man shower, but find the idea of planning daunting? A cottage industry has developed to provide exactly the kind of assistance men need. Sites like ManShower.net organize baby showers for men.

Gift-Giving/Baby Registry Guide

Whether you're throwing a couples' party or a man shower, gifts are usually a big part of the equation. You're not throwing a baby shower just for swag, but guests will not want to show up empty-handed. Parents register for baby presents as a way to take the confusion out of gift giving. Below are some items you may want to include on your list. Each item varies in price and style, and by providing a range of price points, you won't put your guests in an uncomfortable position of only being able to buy expensive gifts off your registry. Some of these gifts are downright essentials, but if these are items you haven't purchased yet, include them. Items essential for the first days with a newborn are marked with an asterisk:

- Stroller*
- Car seat*
- Cradle or co-sleeper*
- Snug-fitting cotton sheets*
- Plastic mattress cover*
- Cloth mattress liners*

- Small cotton blankets*
- T-shirts and onesies*
- Diapers (lots and lots of diapers)*
- Breast pump (if your wife plans to breast-feed)*
- Plastic bottles*
- Formula*
- Diaper bag*
- Digital thermometer*
- Nose syringe*
- Walkers
- Baby backpacks
- Playpen
- Baby lotion
- Pacifiers
- Books
- Stuffed animals
- Diaper disposal unit
- Humidifier
- Baby booties
- Thank-you cards
- Play mats or toys
- Picture frames
- Photo albums

I could go on, but this is a decent list to get you started. If you are attending a baby shower, don't feel pressured to be extravagant in your gifts. But if a couple has put time into creating a registry, try to select something from their list rather than choosing something yourself. This way you'll save the parents time and energy by reducing duplicate gifts so that they don't have to return items from out-of-town stores.

Registering for Gifts Is Harder Than It Sounds

Getting married and having a baby are two of the milestone events in people's lives when it's socially acceptable to create a gift list for well-wishers to purchase for you. Registering when you're engaged is usually fun, but registering while seven months pregnant can be stressful. Kirsten and I registered for baby gifts at Target and Babies "R" Us before Grace was born. Kirsten went to one of the stores with a friend (who didn't have children and unfortunately had zero experience in the matter), and the whole event left her in tears.

Here's what happened: I couldn't go because I was practicing for a game. I wish I could have been there even though I wouldn't have had a clue either. Kirsten said the store was overwhelming, and a sales associate simply handed her a scanner that she was supposed to use throughout the store, scanning merchandise she wanted to add to her registry.

You know what these big-box stores are like—they're hard to navigate on a regular visit, let alone during a pregnancy. Combined with the swirl of hormones, Kirsten couldn't handle it. Faced with seven kinds of breast pumps, not to mention mountains of diapers, swaddling clothes, and bouncy chairs, she left in tears and eventually selected items for her registry online.

At her baby shower, Kirsten received many of the gifts she had added to her registry, but afterward she told me that she wished I could have been there with her. I wasn't there to pick out items for our first child, and I wasn't there when

Kirsten wanted support and love from me. I think that was a pivotal moment. I realized how much I wanted to be there for every part of the pregnancy, and I missed an opportunity. I made up for that fumble with our next babies.

The Takeaway

Whether you host a couples' baby shower or organize a man shower for yourself and your best buddies, the whole point of throwing these parties is to celebrate parenthood. Being part of such events strengthens marital bonds and provides encouragement to hesitant fathers-to-be. Men are more involved in raising children today than they were in previous generations, and with some care, this will be one party you won't want to miss.

CHAPTER EIGHT

Make a Budget

Babies Are Expensive

Doctor's visits, prenatal vitamins, car seats—babies are expensive, even before they're born! The average middle-income American family spends around $12,000 for a baby in the first year of life, and some people spend much more than that. Disposable diapers, baby food, and formula alone can cost nearly $2,500 in the first year![1] Make a list of all the items you will need to purchase (car seat, stroller, crib, bedding, formula, diapers, first aid kit, nursing items), as well as other items you'd like to include, such as birth announcements and toys. If your wife is returning to work, factor in the cost of day care or nanny services as well.

Do you have health insurance? What does it cover? Pay careful attention to what your insurance company will pay for and what you will have to pay for. You do not want to leave the hospital with a precious baby and a massive bill. An uncomplicated, natural (vaginal) delivery may cost around

$11,000, but that varies widely depending on a range of factors, including, for example, where you live.[2]

Do you have life insurance? Pregnancy is life-changing. Does your wife have enough money to take care of the family if you pass away? Or vice versa? It is your parental responsibility to ensure that your family could continue to cope without the income you bring home. Life insurance doesn't have to be expensive, either. You may wish to consider *term life* insurance, which means you only pay for a certain period (or term) of your life.

Maybe, for example, you can afford a twenty-year term life policy—meaning that if you die within those twenty years, your child will have some extra money before he or she turns twenty. Currently, many term life insurance policies for healthy nonsmokers can range between $250 and $350 per year. *Whole life* insurance is exactly what it sounds like—it covers you for your life. It's more expensive, but it also has advantages, especially for families with higher incomes. Free online calculators are available at websites like lifehappens .org. These can help you determine what amount of life insurance is right for you.

Also, staying on this morbid topic of death as we think of the celebration of life, have you put together a will or trust? What happens to your assets if you die? As always, you should consult a financial advisor to examine your particular situation and an attorney to help you put together a will, trust, and perhaps other estate-planning documents.

All I want to impart to you is this: think about how you will care for your child if you are not there. Seek out professional advice from financial planners and attorneys to make sure you've got your family covered. You don't always need a special team on the field, but when you do it's good to know they're available when you're in a tight spot.

And with the prospect of children, we've got to talk about college. Though it's about eighteen years away, consider setting up an education savings plan now. You can invest money tax-free for your child's college in what's called a 529 plan—it's like a 401(k), but instead of covering retirement, it covers college. Contributing as little as $25 each month can make a dent in what may be significant college tuition costs years from now. That sounds like a long way off, doesn't it? Your baby isn't even in your arms yet, but now is the time to prepare. As I mentioned above, talk to a financial planner who can assess your personal situation so that you get the advice you need.

I'm proud to say that we now have our will, trust, and estate plans in order. This was not always the case. Everything takes longer than you think when it comes to these documents. I put it off for a while with every intention of completing them until time kept eluding me. (I'm thankful for a financial planner who kept hounding me!) Once the documents are in place, it is easy to add dependents and beneficiaries as your family grows. With a family of seven, we have had to amend ours quite a few times. There's nothing like the peace of mind when you know you have done your best to secure the financial stability of your family if tragedy should occur. While these documents are important and should be executed, remember the investment of care, love, leadership, faithfulness, and security you give your children and their mother. This is something no amount of money or assets can provide.

If you are the sole breadwinner, you are responsible for the financial health of your family. Thinking about spending money on diapers and preparing for college education can be incredibly stressful for first-time fathers. Remember, the average American family spends nearly $12,000 a year for the first year of a baby's life.

I've been working on my financial game plan with Don Christensen, executive vice president for the Professional Athlete Division of Ronald Blue & Co., a financial advisory firm. For over thirty-five years he has assisted professional athletes by helping them navigate the financial minefields awaiting them, and he once told me this about budgeting and family:

> It's never about the income. It is always about the expenses. That is what you have some control over. Work hard in that area. Spend less than you earn and do it for a long period of time and you will have success with your finances. Start teaching your children early to be stewards. Raise money-smart kids. You create wealth by controlling expenses. Investments are used to preserve what you have saved.

Remember, everything doesn't have to be perfect and you will not have every single baby item that hits the market. While children can be expensive, there is not a specific amount you must have to qualify for parenthood. Don't fall for that lie. A healthy relationship between mother and father creates a loving, nurturing home. That's more important than anything on a registry when it comes to your baby's healthy development. My sister actually slept in a drawer kept on my parents' bedroom floor for a short time when she was born. It was lined with baby blankets, and though it wasn't chic, she turned out great. In fact, she just graduated from college! While we didn't always have everything we wanted growing up, we never lacked the essentials, and we had an abundance of the love, discipline, compassion, and spiritual leadership necessary to turn six rambunctious children into successful adults. My parents trusted God to provide for our needs, and he did. Time flies, you'll see. Budget your time for planning and organizing, and you'll be amazed at how much you accomplish.

PART 3
SUPER BOWL

CHAPTER NINE

Scrimmaging

Last-Minute Preparations

We've covered everything from conception to cravings, and now, approaching the last trimester, it's Super Bowl time! If you weren't ready for your baby's arrival before, then I hate to be the bearer of bad news, but you have a lot of catching up to do. These twelve weeks sprint by, and even if you think there's plenty of time left to pull off a Hail Mary and get everything done, let me be the first to tell you that in my five trips to the delivery room, practice and preparation are crucial. This is not the time to hope that your stellar improvisation skills will keep everyone calm. Consider this chapter your last-chance workout before the big day. In addition to a rundown of what your wife and baby will be experiencing, you'll find checklists to keep you organized and prepared.

The Third Trimester: Weeks 27–40

Back in chapter 5 we briefly discussed what you and your wife may experience during the third trimester. Now let's go into a little more detail about what changes your child is experiencing as the delivery date approaches.

- The baby will put on weight rapidly in this trimester, going from roughly two pounds to nine pounds or more, and growing up to twenty-two inches long. Living space is getting cramped in the womb, meaning the big day is on its way.
- Hair, skin, and nails are no longer transparent.
- *Lanugo*—soft, fine hair that keeps babies warm in utero—begins to shed, as does the *vernix*, a waxy coating that protects the baby from maternal amniotic fluid.
- *Meconium*, also known as baby feces, begins accumulating. What could possibly be in a baby's intestines? It's mostly lanugo, blood cells, and vernix. Meconium is dark green, and you will see it in your baby's first soiled diapers. It's sticky, but it doesn't smell. It's also totally normal.
- The brain will triple in weight in these last weeks, and with this newfound power, the baby has dreams, blinks, and regulates body temperature. Some studies suggest that since maternal hormones cross the placenta, babies may experience stress and other emotions. It's another reason to keep stress levels down and maintain a calm environment.
- All five senses will be fully developed by week thirty. Your wife may notice that loud noises startle the baby.

Studies even suggest that babies recognize their mother's voice.

As you can see, the baby undergoes amazing transformation in the last trimester, and every week in the womb is important for nurturing fetal development.

Premature Birth

Most women give birth around week forty. If the pregnancy reaches forty-two weeks, your doctor will induce labor. If labor occurs before thirty-seven weeks, the baby is considered to be premature. Depending on how early a baby is born, premature delivery can have an impact on the baby's health for years. Only 12 percent of all babies born in America are considered premature. Though doctors aren't always sure what causes preterm labor, a few factors that may contribute to preterm labor include these:

- High blood pressure
- Chronic diseases such as diabetes or heart disease
- Pregnancy in extremely young (under seventeen) or mature (over thirty-five) women
- Infections
- Smoking
- Use of street drugs like cocaine and heroin
- Stress
- Lifting heavy objects
- Lack of proper prenatal care
- Previous miscarriages or abortions

Depending on how early the baby is born, she may not be able to breathe on her own or regulate her own body temperature. Doctors may feed the baby through a nasal tube until she develops the ability to suckle and swallow. These are rare situations, but it's helpful to be aware of them. It's important to remember that despite a few initial challenges, most babies born after twenty-eight weeks eventually thrive.

Your Wife's Body Continues to Evolve

Your wife is experiencing many physical and emotional changes as well. Here are some changes you may notice:

- *Fatigue.* This will intensify, just when your wife needs rest most! Finding comfortable sleeping positions is increasingly difficult. Encourage your wife to eat well and take as many naps as possible. Believe it or not, staying reasonably active may help reduce fatigue as well. Check with your OB/GYN for further suggestions on relieving fatigue.
- *Intense heartburn.* The uterus pushes the mother's stomach upward, and as the baby grows, the amount of space left for the stomach and its contents decreases.
- *Intense dreams.* Your wife may experience vivid dreams, likely caused by the swirl of hormones. Encourage her to write them down or share them with you.
- *Incontinence.* Just as the uterus pushes the stomach upward, it also puts extra weight on the pelvic floor, meaning a sneeze could lead to losing bladder control. Daily *Kegel exercises*, where a woman contracts her

pelvic floor muscles, can help prevent embarrassing leaks. To locate the pelvic floor muscles, she should try to stop urinating midflow—those are the muscles at work. Still unsure? Talk to your doctor.

What specific steps can you take to help your wife through these last few weeks? Since she may find sleeping difficult, if not downright impossible, that body pillow mentioned in chapter 5 may provide temporary relief. Offer her gentle massages and warm compresses to ease her backaches. Though plenty of women welcome the gift of touch, don't be offended if she rejects both; the slightest touch can irritate some women during this delicate stage, so be prepared for either outcome, and don't take it personally.

What to Wear?

Nothing may fit your wife anymore—not even those maternity outfits purchased months earlier, and she may still have her baby shower to attend. Luckily, there are more options for chic maternity wear than ever before. Refer back to chapter 6 to read about Kirsten's maternity photo shoot and the clothes she wore. A white Isabella Oliver sweater provided Kirsten with comfort and style while she enjoyed her first baby shower. She switched it up for Isaiah's shower, wearing a gauzy, stretchy shirt that wrapped around her belly. Remember, possibilities do exist, and with a little detective work, you'll find them. Also, don't be so quick to toss the maternity gear after your wife gives birth. Women's bodies don't snap back to pre-pregnancy shape immediately, so she may want those clothes for months after delivery.

Stress

Expect bouts of stress and anxiety to strike at any moment, even if you've planned for every possible scenario. It's normal to be nervous, especially if you're expecting your first child. I experienced moments of anxiety for all five babies, and I'm a reformed perfectionist! Try to remember that you are prepared and that you will get through this.

Labor and Delivery Day Checklist

At least one month prior to delivery day, pack your overnight bags so that you'll be ready at a moment's notice to head to the hospital. Kirsten and I had ours organized and packed months in advance, but that's just what worked for us. I would advise you to pack early too—it's always better to be prepared.

Here's what you will most likely need during your visit to the hospital:

- Nursing gown
- Baby outfit (T-shirt or onesie; sleepers if the weather is cold)
- Cotton blanket for swaddling
- Car seat (the hospital won't let you leave without one but may not help install it due to liability issues)
- Insurance card
- Hospital paperwork

- Birth plan
- Toiletries

The following items certainly aren't essentials but can help with waiting, documenting the birth, or keeping in touch with family and friends:

- iPad and charger
- Books or magazines
- Camera
- Breast pump (some hospitals provide temporary pumps; be sure to check ahead)
- Snacks and electrolyte drinks (I brought a twelve-pack of Frost Riptide Rush Gatorade—Kirsten's favorite)

While it may be tempting to bring more items, I caution against it. I've heard of parents bringing champagne, only to be too tired to uncork the bottle and having to haul the bubbly back home. Remember, you're bringing a baby home too, so less is best.

Final Nursery Preparations

You won't have the time or the energy to put together a crib or wash loads of onesies after the baby arrives. Plan on having the following items set up and ready for use at least one month before the delivery date. Here's a pro tip: start tackling the list during the second trimester. Pick one project per weekend, so it's not overwhelming.

Some of the items with prior assembly required include the following:

- Crib: For safety, select a crib with slats less than 2⅜ inches across, with a snug-fitting mattress and child-proof locks. Cribs should not have any sharp edges or corner posts that stick up—clothing can snag on edges and trap or suffocate a baby. Do not use any crib manufactured prior to 1975 unless all the paint has been stripped off. Paint used prior to 1975 often contained lead, so think carefully before using the family heirloom for your baby. Keep cloth bumpers and toys out of the crib for now—they are suffocation hazards.
- Changing table
- Diaper disposal unit
- High chair
- Rocker/glider
- Stroller
- Car seat: Visit www.dmv.org/how-to-guides/install-child-seat.php for step-by-step instructions on how to install a car seat correctly. Check out www.safercar.gov/cpsApp/cps/index.htm as well. It provides a search program that identifies child safety seat inspection stations in your area. Remember: seven out of ten child safety seats are not installed correctly, and car crashes are one of the leading causes of death for children between one and thirteen years old. Car seats save lives! Since 1975, car seats have saved more than 9,600 children from dying in car crashes.[1] For further guidance, the American Society of Pediatrics publishes a booklet called "The Family Shopping Guide to Car Seats," available online.

Top Three Must-Haves and Tiny Keepsakes

After shepherding five children into the world, Kirsten and I have narrowed the list of must-haves down to three items, in addition to a car seat. Make sure you have a breast pump if your wife is breast-feeding, a stroller for transporting the baby wherever you go, and a co-sleeper for when the baby first arrives. These items will make it easier to return to regular daily activities with a baby in tow.

Though not essential, you may consider booking a maternity photo shoot, having a 3-D or 4-D ultrasound, or even creating a 3-D plaster cast of your wife's belly. We ordered 3-D images of our babies, and Kirsten had her belly cast when she was pregnant with Grace. I found the belly kit interesting, and the result was this convex mold of Kirsten's stomach. We displayed ours for a while, but after moving so many times we tucked it carefully away for safekeeping. Check online for artists who specialize in the process, or, if you're the creative type, you can do it yourself with belly cast kits, available from big-box stores like Target and Amazon. Each of these keepsakes serves as a sweet reminder of this entire experience long after the baby arrives.

Washing Onesies

All those adorable onesies, undershirts, and pajamas must be washed prior to wear. Newborns have sensitive skin that is easily irritated by manufacturing chemicals and perfumes. Washing also makes the clothes softer and prevents skin rashes. You don't need specific baby detergent, but use a gentle cleaner that has no dye or perfumes. Dreft is a tried-and-true liquid cleanser that is safe for newborns, and you can't miss the bubblegum-pink bottles in the detergent aisle at the grocery store. It can get expensive, however. Alternatives include Arm & Hammer Sensitive Skin and All Free and Clear. Be sure to follow all washing directions.

Continuing Education

Have you attended any childbirth classes yet? If this is your first child, I highly recommend you do. The hands-on practice will help reduce stress and anxiety while also providing guidance for this glorious event about to occur. Hospitals and private practitioners offer many types of classes. Ask your friends and family for recommendations about different classes, and your health insurance company may provide suggestions as well. There are even online courses now. Make sure that the childbirth class you are considering lines up with your birth plan and philosophy. Though they're all different, childbirth classes have the same goal of providing tools and techniques to make the delivery process as smooth and stress-free as possible.

No matter what kind of class you choose, you'll find many of the following topics on the agenda:

- How to swaddle your baby (I was king of the "DUDU" swaddle method, and swaddling is critical for keeping newborns calm and warm.)
- Diapering
- Administering infant CPR
- Breast-feeding techniques and the importance of the "monster chomp" and latch

- Basic newborn care
- C-section and induction explanations
- Managing pain
- Labor stages
- Labor positions to relieve pain and line baby up with pelvis
- Breathing techniques

Finalize the Birth Plan

We talked about a birth plan in chapter 2, and now is a good time to review it or create one if you haven't already. In addition to the items from chapter 2, consider addressing the following:

- Pain management
- Music
- Lighting
- Aromatherapy
- Cutting the umbilical cord (I cut all five.)
- Delivering the baby (I delivered our last two babies.)

As you can see, there's plenty left to tackle before the baby arrives. I'm so glad I made it to the prenatal classes with Kirsten, and that we had time to assemble the nursery before Grace's arrival. After delivery your life will go into overdrive, so don't put off till tomorrow what you can do today.

CHAPTER TEN

Game Day

Labor, Delivery, and Your First Moments with Your Child

The big day has finally arrived. The moment you and your wife have spent the past nine months preparing and planning for is here. By now you've figured out your birth plan and selected a doctor, and are on your way to the hospital. You and your wife have a great deal to say about how your child arrives into this world. Below I've outlined a few tips and suggestions to ensure you have a successful game day. And with five kids, I'll share my own experiences to help guide you toward the best plan for your family.

Childbirth and Modern Medicine: All the Ways to Deliver a Baby

First, a quick word about your birth plan: Childbirth is safer now than ever before in recorded history, but that doesn't exclude the unexpected from occurring. You may have developed the ideal birth plan, found the perfect doctor, and attended all the right birthing classes, but sometimes, whether on the field or in life, things don't go according to plan. Some of your birth plan requests may not be accommodated if the health of the mother or child is at risk. Remember that although you are a vital part of the delivery process, you are not a doctor. You may feel a little let down, but don't take it personally if the doctor decides that a particular part of your birth plan is unsafe. Do understand that decision was made with the health of your wife and child as the top priority. The goal is to deliver a healthy child. Each of my children's deliveries was a totally different experience, so I can share some personal insight on the different methods of delivering babies.

Medicated Labor

If your wife elected to have an *epidural*, an injection of an anesthetic into the spinal cord, make sure to ask for the head anesthesiologist—you don't want any second-stringers playing around with this. When Kirsten was delivering Grace, the assistant had trouble administering the epidural. I was getting quite agitated watching Kirsten jump as he moved the needle back and forth in her spine. Seeing that I was on the verge of exploding, the nurse offered to get the head anesthesiologist. We both thought that was a great idea for everyone involved! The head anesthesiologist placed it with no problem, and the epidural provided comfort, yet Kirsten was still able to push through her contractions.

With Naomi, we were sure to get the head anesthesiologist, but we found out that not all drug cocktails are created equal.

This time around, Kirsten was throwing up, her blood pressure dropped drastically, and as a result, much of our birth plan went right out the window. Although our experiences with Grace and Naomi were in different hospitals, you can be in the same hospital, have the same doctor, use the same birth plan, and still have a completely different experience. Naomi arrived safely, but the process was vastly different than with Grace.

The benefit to having an epidural is that when it works, the pain is lessened, and the mother feels calm and more relaxed during the delivery process. This option is not without side effects, though. Longer labor, fetal monitoring, immobility, and other interventions like catheters and the use of the drug Pitocin may accompany the choice to have an epidural. And as Kirsten experienced, each epidural can be different, so it's important to be prepared for this uncertainty. Talk to your doctor so that you understand all the risks associated with medicated labor for the mother as well as your soon-to-be-born baby.

Sometimes a Caesarean section, or C-section, is performed to remove the baby from the uterus. This may be the result of complications during labor or may be planned. During a C-section the baby will be surgically removed through an incision in the mother's abdomen and a second incision in the uterus. The entire procedure usually takes between 60 and 120 minutes, but the mother can expect to stay in the hospital for two to four days. Expect a longer recovery than with a vaginal birth and more restrictions on daily activity. Also, since a C-section is major surgery, be alert for complications like excessive bleeding and infection.

Natural Birth, Doulas, and Midwives

Kirsten gave birth to our next two children in the natural birthing ward of a hospital without medical intervention, and Eden was born at home. A *natural birth* is when a woman elects to go through the birthing process with minimal medical or technological intervention, particularly anesthesia, and focuses on breathing techniques, relaxation, and other forms of natural pain management. To help manage pain and focus on delivering a child, some women hire doulas or midwives to help them through the process. Derived from the Greek word for "woman's helper," a *doula* is a trained, nonmedical professional whose goal is to provide laboring women continuous support until the baby is born. Sometimes doulas assist in caring for the newborn too. Doulas reassure and soothe laboring women when the going gets tough, and might be helpful if your wife has decided to go for a natural childbirth without anesthesia. Aromatherapy, massage, and even hair pulling are a few methods doulas employ to support your wife as she transitions through each stage of labor.

Don't feel threatened by a doula's presence. They are not there to replace you; they actually encourage fathers to provide loving support instead of stressing out or coaching their wife through breathing techniques. The website www.dona.org is a great resource if you're considering hiring a doula. Studies have demonstrated that doulas reduce the likelihood a woman will need an epidural or undergo a Caesarean section.[1] Do your research before hiring one, and make sure your OB/GYN is on call in case circumstances change.

Over 15,000 practicing midwives provide maternity and postpartum care throughout all fifty states. A *midwife* is a health-care provider. Midwives are usually trained as nurses, then complete graduate coursework in midwifery. All midwives must pass a nationally administered exam. They are licensed practitioners, can diagnose illnesses and prescribe medications, and can deliver in a home setting or in a hospital. Many midwives work with a dedicated physician or OB/GYN as well. Some women choose to have midwives as their primary gynecological care provider. Midwives and doulas often work together when orchestrating a natural delivery—the midwife executes the birth plan, and the doula provides coaching and support.

Kirsten hired a doula and a midwife for her last three deliveries. Her midwife and doula were total professionals and provided counseling, care, and support in a calm yet empowering manner. They helped Kirsten realize that what she was experiencing was normal and natural, and that they would encourage her through the process. After her difficult experience with the epidural during Naomi's delivery, she was ready to try a different option. The natural births ended up being beautiful, not sterile, and her postpartum recovery was much faster than when she had an epidural.

Whether your wife goes natural or has an epidural, it's a lot of work. Natural births are definitely more exhausting, but if epidurals go according to plan, they are amazing. Take it from a lady who's done it all, and consider all the options when it comes to what your wife thinks will work best for her.

To Look, or Not to Look?

When you are by your wife's side in the delivery room, you'll probably still be deciding whether or not to look at your baby during the actual delivery. Everyone is different. I just knew that I would watch Grace being born, and I watched all of our children arrive in the world. In all honesty, I was kind of nervous about looking. I already knew I was going to be in the room, coaching and soothing her and saying what she needed to hear, but I took each decision down to the wire—flip-flopping until the second the baby made her entrance.

While Kirsten was pregnant with Grace, I remember having a conversation about watching the actual delivery with a Patriots teammate who had three kids already, and I was hemming and hawing about whether to look or not. He said, "I never looked. If I looked, it would change my relationship with my wife forever." So he never did. I did, and my relationship didn't change with Kirsten. I felt that such a moment is precious, and I didn't want to miss it. Either way, your child is coming. Perhaps the best advice I can give is to do what you think is right for you and your spouse—there's no right or wrong answer.

For me, one of the benefits of experiencing natural birth was being able to participate in the delivery process. I actually delivered my last two children. They were both *water births*, meaning Kirsten labored in a tub specifically designated for delivery.

A word of caution about water births—do not attempt to give birth in a hot tub or whirlpool. This can cause severe dehydration and put the lives of mother and child at risk. Natural water births should only occur under the supervision of a trained health-care provider.

I first asked if I could participate in the water birth of my children, and Kirsten's midwife was agreeable to letting me guide the baby out of the birth canal. She warned me that I would have to move fast when the time came.

As birth became imminent and the baby started to crown, the midwife told me to get into position. Sometimes babies rock back and forth in the canal as the mother pushes, and the midwife or the OB/GYN knows when it's time to start guiding the baby's head out of the canal. It was then that the midwife told me to get ready. I had been kneeling beside the tub with my arms around Kirsten, encouraging her and breathing with her. When the midwife called me, I came around the front and put my arms in the water, grasping the baby's head. Kirsten made one last effort, and as I gently supported the head after delivering the shoulders, the baby came tumbling out. Next, I placed the baby directly on Kirsten's chest, after which I cut the umbilical cord. It was amazing, and I am so happy I did it. I wasn't ready to do it with Grace, but by baby number four I couldn't let the opportunity pass me by.

Congratulations! Holding Your Baby for the First Time and Finding Spiritual Strength

Holding your child for the first time is an unbelievable experience. You may feel elation, fear, fatigue, or a combination of all three. I felt an intense sense of responsibility every time I cradled my babies for the first time. I was grateful to God for giving me a healthy child and the opportunity to raise a baby who would someday grow into someone who loves the Lord wholeheartedly. I also felt scared! How could I, an imperfect man, be the father and husband my family needed me to be? I am so thankful for God's grace that covers my shortcomings.

Once my children come home, my top priority as a father is to continue to grow close to Christ so that I can effectively spend the next eighteen years guiding and raising my children to recognize their need for him. I have those years to steer them toward God, to teach them his truth, and to demonstrate my daily devotion to him through my marriage and my daily life. By leading a godly life, I hope that my children will also devote their lives to the Lord, and that as adults they will continue living for him.

Accepting Our Roles as Fathers and as Imperfect Beings in the Eyes of the Lord

When I hold my children for the first time, I also see their potential to change the world, and not simply to create justice out of injustice, but through everyday acts of kindness—feeding the hungry, providing solace and comfort to others, and promoting peace and serenity. Perhaps my children will grow up to become Christian leaders, guiding and challenging the pervading culture through words and action, or perhaps they will do God's work by being great friends and teammates to others. I feel the weight of having to mold and instruct these children, while still understanding that it is the Holy Spirit who must draw their hearts toward him. That's my job as a parent. These kids aren't ours alone; they belong to God. Kirsten and I are simply the stewards of these little lives God has entrusted to us. At some point, I'm going to have to stand before God and answer the question, "What did you do with what I gave you?" And that includes how well I guided his children.

That may sound like an overwhelming burden, but I think it's all about perspective. It's about understanding and living in a state of grace. I understand that I'm not a perfect parent because I'm not a perfect person. No one is. I also understand that I'm not going to raise a perfect child because my children are the product of sin and will act the same way I did, and still do. They will go through periods of rebellion, talk back, be hateful and lustful, just like me. I see myself in my children—on the one hand, I'm here to lead and to guide them, and on the other hand, they reveal to me my own need for repentance, forgiveness, and salvation.

For example, my three-year-old son Judah gets into all sorts of mischief, and although he may make me upset sometimes, I have to laugh, because when I see him, I see me at his age. And through that, I understand that God's grace is sufficient for my shortcomings as a parent, which pushes me to rely on him for the strength and the wisdom to lead my children. Remember, we are all imperfect. We will have our moments of poor judgment and will succumb to weakness and temptation. I will not be the perfect embodiment of a man, or of a father, or of a Christian. What I am is a man who is imperfect and fallen, in need of a savior. That's what I hope my children will learn as they grow. Kirsten and I are imperfect, and we are forever striving to grow and learn from our hardships and our mistakes. We believe that to live is Christ, and our hope is that through repentance and faith our children will live for Christ as well.

PART 4

POSTGAME

CHAPTER ELEVEN

Monday Morning Quarterback

The Baby's Home, Now What?

During the first week back at home, it's safe to say that your life has drastically changed. You might be too exhausted to understand the extent of that change, but it has—and for the better. You are home with your new baby, and life will take on a whole new meaning. In the meantime, you've done your part in preparing the nest by ensuring that there is food in the refrigerator, your socks and boxers are not scattered all over the floor, and any bills are paid so that you can focus entirely on caring for your new bundle and your wife.

The nine months of pregnancy are behind you now, and you've got to figure out how to keep two people happy and comfortable. Your wife's body will be readjusting to life postpartum, and your baby will make leaps and bounds in growth and development. Remember to take deep breaths and to take one day at a time. Here's what you can expect in these first sleepless days.

Hospital Discharge and the First Days at Home

After Grace was born, I was ready to hop into the car and take everyone home. However, new mothers and their children generally spend one or two days in the hospital unless there are complications. Kirsten loved those days in the hospital. She could sleep almost as much as she wanted because Grace spent time in the nursery. I slept on the uncomfortable guest couch, but we were able to build up our strength for the sleepless nights that waited for us at home. With the subsequent children, I was shuttling them back and forth to the hospital, so it wasn't as restful. My point is this: get as much rest as you can, when you can get it.

Though Kirsten had no problems nursing Grace in the hospital, she ran into trouble when we were heading home. Although Grace hadn't cried at all during the entire hospital stay, she went ballistic as soon as we pulled out of the hospital driveway. Kirsten and I were worried something was terribly wrong. Grace was latching on, but Kirsten's milk hadn't come in yet, so we were concerned that she wasn't getting the nutrients she needed. So we started giving Grace small amounts of formula through a syringe for a day for our peace of mind. Kirsten and I were scared because the baby wasn't growing like we thought she should, and Kirsten thought she was doing something wrong.

This was our firstborn, and I wasn't sure how everything was going to play out, but I just kept repeating to her, "Baby, it's going to be all right. Grace will eat. She will get healthy.

We will get her there." Though I was providing reassurance, inside I was terrified. At that moment, the weight of responsibility hit me like a ton of bricks. The truth was, I didn't know how everything would turn out, and we hadn't planned for this scenario. There were no nurses to guide us anymore. We were like two sailors in a rowboat sailing across the Atlantic without a compass.

In any event, Kirsten was set on breast-feeding and she ultimately breast-fed all our children until they were a year old. But breast-feeding didn't come easily with Grace. There were times when Kirsten's nipples bled, and she was in terrible pain as she tried to feed our child. Though she persevered, sometimes we had to say to ourselves that it was okay to take a break when Kirsten's body needed it. Kirsten didn't want to give Grace formula, but Grace needed nourishment, and we decided apprehensively to give her formula until everything calmed down and Kirsten was able to reestablish a rhythm. Finally, Kirsten and I got into a routine where she pumped milk and I would take over a nighttime feeding so that she could sleep a little. Luckily, this was the off-season so I could help out.

Like many nursing mothers, Kirsten made a routine out of pumping additional bottles of milk after or between feedings. She would fill tubes with breast milk and put them in the freezer. Sometimes I took care of the night feedings. I would take out a couple tubes of milk and put them in an insulated case that I kept by my bedside, so that they would thaw but not spoil. Upon hearing that 2:00 a.m. wail, I'd get up and feed Grace. Though it felt like it took hours for Grace's tiny lips to suck those few ounces of milk in the wee hours of the morning, I developed a new appreciation for what Kirsten did every day and most nights when Grace was hungry.

The first days at home were different with each child. The time of year they were born determined how much I could help out. Isaiah was born in October, right in the middle of the season, and I felt guilty because I missed out on so much of the first days of his life. I couldn't wake up in the middle of the night to help out with feedings or diaper changes. Kirsten understood and said to me, "You need to sleep in the other room. Get your rest for work." I agreed, but a part of me felt like I wasn't doing my part and struggling alongside her.

You may find that your job will prevent you from participating as much as you might like. Have a conversation with your wife about how much you can realistically help out, and if your wife needs additional support, consider asking family members or babysitters to lend a hand. Kirsten's mother and my mother each spent two separate weeks with us, and though they didn't get up to do nighttime feedings, they did take the morning and some afternoon shifts so that Kirsten could catch up on her sleep. Recruit your family to your team when you can—everyone gets to bond with the newborn, and having people to lean on provides strength and encouragement.

It is vitally important that you act as a gatekeeper during these first few weeks. Friends and family will be excited about the new addition and will want to visit to get their first glimpse. Have a conversation about who can visit and when. It is critical that your wife be able to rest and not entertain if she doesn't want to. She may feel pressured to oblige, but assure her that her health and the baby's health are a priority right now. Entertaining guests may have to wait.

The Zombie Stage

Before I had kids, I thought I knew fatigue. I'd come home after work, plop on the couch, not move for hours, and play video games. After children, I discovered a whole new dimension of fatigue that I didn't know existed. No one can prepare you for that amount of exhaustion, because it's not just about your fatigue. You have to push through because another life depends on you. There is no room for error or to indulge in a nap when you want. Newborns wake up every few hours, and as a result, you don't sleep soundly because you have to be ready for anything at any time—in the middle of the night, early in the morning, or at four in the afternoon. Maybe you're a pro sleeper, snoring through thunderstorms and romantic movies, but recent studies have demonstrated that new fathers have elevated levels of cortisol and prolactin, the same hormones present in new mothers. These hormones correspond to greater connectivity, meaning you're predisposed to sleep lightly with a newborn in the house.[1]

I'm not just talking about one sleepless night—anyone can go all night, maybe even two nights in a row. After that, sleep deprivation takes its toll. Get three weeks into life with a newborn, and sleep deprivation changes your mood, judgment, and even physical strength. I remember even getting angry at the baby and thinking, *Why won't you just sleep?* Grace was up every few hours for the first four months until she developed a day-night sleep pattern. The first time she slept through the night, Kirsten and I woke up asking if the other had fed Grace already. Rather than immediate elation, we ran into Grace's room to see if everything was all right. Of course she was fine, and we had reached another milestone, but we were so used to running on no sleep that we weren't prepared for it.

And every baby is different: Naomi wanted to be held all the time—no bassinets or cribs for her. Only someone's loving arms would do. Even though babies don't weigh much at the beginning, it becomes a strain, and Naomi cried all the time! I remember one time when I was so upset that I had to pass the baby off to Kirsten. And I was angry at myself for being angry. There were other times when I would come home and Kirsten would silently pass the baby off to me because she was so exhausted and needed to take a break. I was tired, but I did it because I was concerned only with our child's health and Kirsten's well-being. My fatigue took a backseat.

A Range of Emotions

As you can see, nothing really prepares you for the baby's homecoming, and it won't all be joy and bliss. You will get angry, frustrated, and sad. After the initial joy wears off, reality will set in. Think of your wedding day—it was amazing. Then you had to work to keep your marriage running like a well-oiled machine, and that is what makes a marriage beautiful. It's not something that you set on autopilot and forget. Marriage requires work, just like child-rearing. There's sacrifice involved in each situation. There will be times when you won't like your spouse, and she'll feel the same way, but if you're able to work through the tough times, put pride in your back pocket, and talk through your problems, you will succeed. Child-rearing is the same. You're not going to be pleased with your child 100 percent of the time. That child will test your limits and will do exactly the opposite of what you ask, because that's what children do. Babies will frustrate you because you can't decipher whether that piercing wail means they need more food or another cuddle. I can't recount all the times I was frustrated because the baby wouldn't go to sleep. It would be two thirty in the morning, and Grace would be fed, her diaper clean, and she would still be crying! She didn't want her swing, she was unhappy in the co-sleeper, and she was just being a normal, fussy little baby.

I've even yelled, "Go to sleep!" and felt guilty immediately afterwards. Then I would get even more upset because the baby had no idea what I was saying! Remember, rational thought can be influenced by sleep deprivation, and for a nanosecond I believed yelling at a newborn would work. I remember putting Grace in her co-sleeper and saying, "I'm going to sleep even if you don't." Well, that didn't work either. The zombie stage is rough, but it's important to understand that you will feel this range of emotions, and that it's common for parents to feel upset or even helpless.

When to Get Help—Shaken Baby Syndrome

We've all heard horror stories of parents shaking their babies, and it's important to recognize what causes this and how to avoid shaken baby syndrome. *Shaken baby syndrome* is the medical term that describes injuries resulting from shaking an infant. It is a form of abuse and can lead to permanent injury or death. Usually shaken baby syndrome happens when a parent or caregiver is frustrated or angry because a child won't stop crying. The parent or caregiver will shake the baby, which may cause the child to stop crying for a while. Abusers see that the shaking stops the crying, and a pattern develops, resulting in subsequent attacks. There are few external signs of shaken baby syndrome, but internal injuries can be severe.

Shaken baby syndrome can result in the following:

- Brain swelling
- Brain damage
- Hemorrhaging
- Mental retardation
- Developmental issues
- Blindness
- Hearing loss
- Paralysis
- Death

Frustration and anger are normal, but if you ever reach the point where you think you may shake your baby, take the following steps:

- Provide a pacifier.
- Try a different sleeping position (co-sleeper, crib).
- Play "white noise," a steady, unobtrusive sound, like running the vacuum, humidifier, television static, or our favorite, the sound machine.
- Gently hug or cuddle the baby.

If this doesn't work, and you're still feeling frustrated, place the baby in a safe place like a crib. Remember, a baby cannot injure herself from crying. Take a break, even if the baby is still crying. If another adult isn't around, call someone you trust. There are many anonymous hotlines you can call as well, like the US National Parent Helpline at 1-855-4A PARENT (427-2736), the 24-Hour Parent Helpline at 1-888-435-7553, or the Fussy Baby Warmline at 1-888-431-BABY. If you think you or your baby are in immediate danger, call 911.

Over three hundred babies die every year due to complications from shaken baby syndrome, and thousands more live with lifelong, irreversible injuries as a result.

Never shake your baby. Let me say that again: Never shake your baby. The results could be permanent.

Lend a Hand—Parenting Is Real Work

It's important for fathers to help out when they can and as their schedule allows. It helps create a bond between father and child, and you'll be able to empathize with your wife because you're experiencing similar situations like sleep deprivation and bonding. I've talked to men who say, "All my wife does is stay at home with the kids. She has it so easy. It's not real work." I mostly hear this from guys who don't lift a finger around the house, who haven't changed a diaper, and who haven't awakened to do the 3:00 a.m. feeding. They haven't cleaned spit-up or cradled a fussy newborn when they'd much prefer rolling over and going back to sleep. It is real work, and if you take time to be part of the process, you'll have a greater understanding for how much your wife is doing to raise happy and healthy children.

Changing Diapers and Finding Your Game Mode

To the men out there who have never changed a diaper, I've got news for you: if you are invested in raising a healthy family, you will change diapers. Growing up, I changed a few diapers for at least three of my five siblings, so changing Grace's diapers was like riding a bicycle. I know there are men who say, "Not a chance!" But when it's your child, you will be surprised by your focus and willingness to do it. Sure, before you had kids, you thought, *That's gross! Baby poop smells terrible.* Afterward, if you are committed to your family, that attitude changes, or at least it should. There will be times when you have poop dripping down your arm or exploding out the sides of a diaper onto everything nearby, and you are not going to turn on your heels and run out of the room. You are going to suck it up and finish the job because you care for your child. That is what I call finding your game mode.

I loved changing my children's diapers. The smell never bothered me, at least during the first year. As babies age, those diapers are a different story! In any event, I'm focused on the intimacy of the situation. This tiny, totally dependent being is right in front of me, and there's nothing he or she can do. In a way, it is a poignant reminder of God's forgiveness. He cleans up our mess, our sin that we cannot cleanse, and gives us a new heart. It's a gift your child cannot repay, but you do it out of kindness and love. I never regretted those moments. Look, I couldn't nurse, I certainly couldn't give birth, but the one sure thing I could do was change diapers. So every diaper I could change, I did. It was my way of being involved.

Would I ever want to watch someone else's child be born, or willingly clean up after another child's accident? No, but when it's your family, you do it. Just the other day, my son was sick—projectile vomiting everywhere. I had a unique opportunity to use my professional skills at home and actually caught the vomit, then helped him to the bathroom. I didn't even think about it. It's just what you do. My hope is that something will click automatically when it's your kid who's sick or needs a fresh diaper. And afterward, sure, take a break to reflect on how unpleasant it was. But like the famous sneaker company's motto says, just do it.

Baby's First Bath

Get your camera ready, because giving your baby his or her first bath is a monumental occasion. Babies used to be bathed right after birth; however, new research shows that delaying a newborn's first bath reduces the risk of infection, stabilizes infant blood sugar, and improves parent-infant bonding.[2] Now, it's normal to wait at least forty-eight hours, if not longer, before giving a bath. Be sure to find out what your hospital's practice is regarding bathing. If your hospital still bathes right after birth, you can request that the doctors wait.

The vernix is still on the baby's skin, and acts as a natural moisturizer and protectant. Vernix also provides protection as babies become accustomed to living in an air-filled environment rather than being surrounded by amniotic fluid. That new baby smell is from vernix.

Your baby's first bath will not be in a full-size tub. You've probably got an infant tub waiting for you. If you don't have one, you can put the baby in the sink, but be extremely careful around the faucet. Infant tubs are better because they help prop up newborns and provide greater stability than the amenities in a sink. Newborns are slippery! When you do finally get to wash your baby, remember the following:

- Don't submerge the baby.
- Use a little bit of baby soap, if at all. Newborns aren't exactly playing in the mud.
- Use no more than two inches of water until you become comfortable bathing your child.
- Heat the water to body temperature—90 to 100 degrees Fahrenheit. If you're unsure how hot is too hot, use a bath thermometer, and always test the temperature with your elbow or wrist. It should be comfortable, never hot. (There are even floating thermometers for baby baths that turn different colors depending on temperature.)
- Hold your baby so that your forearm supports the head while the fingers of that cradling hand hold the baby by the armpit.
- Using a soft washcloth and without soap, gently wash the baby's face.
- Next, wash the rest of the baby's body—arms, legs, and genitals—without soap at first. When you do use soap, lather your hands rather than the washcloth. It's easier that way.
- Keep one hand on the baby at all times.
- Blot dry rather than rub, especially if the navel is not completely healed yet. Use cotton balls to dab the navel dry.
- Do not stick cotton swabs into the ears to clean out wax.
- Baby lotion is generally unnecessary. If you do use baby lotion, choose an unscented brand.
- Don't worry about those blue-gray, blue-black, or deep brown splotches your baby may have on his bottom and back. These congenital birthmarks are called *Mongolian*

spots and usually disappear within the first four years of life.

Also—and this is critical—never leave the baby alone in the tub. Babies can drown in less than an inch of water.

I remember Grace's first bath. I have the pictures to remind me. There she was, in the infant tub, barely two weeks old, and totally luxuriating in the experience. Your baby may be frightened at first—babies can sense when you're nervous—but with time and practice, bath time has the potential of becoming a fun ritual. Bath time is bonding time.

Bath time can also remain a great bonding opportunity as your child grows. It becomes the highlight of their day, especially when they're still young. I still enjoy bathing the kids. At six and seven, the girls are graduating to bathing themselves, but I still enjoy the daily ritual with my boys, who are three and four. Sometimes it's easier to take the baby in the shower with me, especially when we're vacationing, whether we're staying at a hotel or at their grandparents' house. It's a quick affair: lather, rinse, then a quick handoff to Kirsten holding a fluffy towel. I actually have a picture of bath time from when we visited Kirsten's grandmother when Grace was a baby. It's a sweet memento that reminds me how precious every minute is with my children. Even though they are getting older, the kids still get excited during bath time. It's not the same as when they were babies, but it's our time to connect. Sometimes I play music on my cell phone—it's like a big party! "Pretty Brown Eyes" by Mint Condition is a frequent bath-time request. It's our moment in the day to catch up, and it won't last forever. Enjoy it while you can.

Skin to Skin and Bonding

Babies love to be touched. They're surrounded by their mothers in the womb, and it's only natural that they crave that same feeling after they're born. For millennia, women have carried their babies all day long, toting them from place to place, breast-feeding at a second's notice. In the United States those traditional child-rearing practices were largely displaced by nurseries, cribs, and strollers. Happily, new studies demonstrate that babies thrive when in regular physical contact, and the act of touch releases relaxation and happiness hormones in the brain.[3] Some experts have even suggested that if parents don't bond with their children in the first forty-eight hours, then the opportunity is lost. While every opportunity is important, parents can always strive to make up for lost time. The fact remains, though, that regular, consistent periods of caresses, kisses, and hugs are the building blocks of parent-child bonding.

I was fortunate to spend at least some time at home with the babies after they were born, holding them on my chest and feeling their tiny hearts beating. It's time you'll never get back, so if you're nervous about bonding, allow yourself the opportunity to create that emotional attachment with your child. They'll be healthier for it, and so will you.

Avoiding Paternal Resentment

As I've mentioned throughout the book, fathers have an important role to play in the pregnancy process, but once that first baby arrives, it's clear as day that the family dynamic has shifted, and it's no longer all about you and your wife.

Everything revolves around protecting and nurturing that baby. It's possible you may begin to feel resentment towards the baby. It's pretty common. Be an active participant so that you don't feel alienated.

When we brought Grace home, I resented the time the baby took away from Kirsten and me, but as days passed I realized that those were misplaced emotions. In fact, I've felt that way with all my children, even though I know what to expect. Don't be stubborn and act tough like me. Instead, communicate with your wife, because she needs to know how you feel. She may not validate those emotions, because, let's be honest, if you're complaining that you don't have enough alone time with your wife while she's caring for a newborn, you sound awfully selfish. But that doesn't mean that you can't remind her that your bond still counts. Kirsten is very perceptive, and she could sense when I was feeling left out. Unfortunately, that created another burden for her—how to maintain that bond with me while caring for the baby. Once I swallowed my pride, we finally talked it out, and I grew as a father and a husband.

Bonding and Returning to Work

Many mothers who continue to have professional careers away from the home often find themselves in the unfortunate position of having to return to work sooner than they'd like. As a result, these mothers worry that by going back to work too soon, they'll miss out on the early milestone moments and lose their bond with the baby. The truth is that you can't be everywhere with them all the time. Time missed with your children is just that. It's a tough decision. But babies will love their parents and bond with them even if they have different caregivers during the week. That's what evenings, weekends, and vacations are for.

I have spoken with some parents who are reluctant to form bonds with their newborns out of the fear that they will have to break that attachment when they go back to work. Whether you or your wife are willing or financially able to take off extra time from work is ultimately your decision. However, if you can spend the first four months with your baby, you or your wife will be more likely to return to work feeling secure in your relationship with your child.[4]

CHAPTER TWELVE

Keeping the Marital Bonds Strong

We've covered a lot of ground so far. By now, you should be comfortable taking care of your child and doing your part around the house. In the middle of all that, it's important not to forget about your relationship with your wife. For almost a year, everything you and your wife have been doing has been with the sole purpose of bringing a healthy child into the world. Now that the baby is here, you've got another task ahead of you: strengthening your bond with your wife. Having a baby brought Kirsten and me closer together in the long run, but lack of sleep and poor communication caused some hurt feelings along the way. We got through it. Here's how to bring the spark back to your relationship too.

Six Weeks Postpartum: Make a Date

You and your wife are in this together. Physically, spiritually, and emotionally, you are one. You're not going against each other, and you've got to be in sync with each other's needs. I'm willing to bet that your date nights have probably fallen to the bottom of your priority list while you've both been busy changing diapers, doing round-the-clock feedings, and adjusting to life with a newborn. Still, couples need time alone together. It's important to reestablish your intimacy with your wife, but be aware that you might have to take it slow. The first six weeks postpartum will be hectic, and many mothers develop an intense maternal bond with their child, to the exclusion of intimacy with everyone else—including you. Your wife may feel guilty at the thought of taking an evening away from her baby, and you may feel the same. And yet you may both feel guilty that you're not engaging with each other like you were before the baby was born.

And while you will probably have to wait four to six weeks postpartum before engaging in sex, you can still reignite the fire you have for each other in different ways. We talked about this earlier, but you have to know the love language that best fits the mother of your child. It is your job to know whether she feels loved and valued when you do household chores, give her gifts, touch the small of her back, or tell her what a great job she is doing as a mother. Being intentional in this area is critical during the first postpartum months, when time as a couple is at an all-time low. This may be a shocker to some readers out there, but sex is only a small part of intimacy. With the right attitude, you may discover real intimacy during this time that sex is on the shelf.

As our babies got older, we always made it a priority to get date night back on the calendar. It doesn't have to be anything fancy—perhaps you just want to go to your favorite local diner and sit in a booth. Finding time for each other gives you a few moments to relax and reboot. Here are a few tips to make date night a success:

- Enlist the help of local grandparents or aunts and uncles. They'll be thrilled to spend some quality one-on-one time with the baby, and extended family can have a positive impact on children's emotional development.
- Pick a spot that you and your wife both enjoy.
- See a play or a movie.
- Take an outdoor hike without the baby.
- Indulge in a spa day.
- No matter what you decide to do, put it on the calendar.
- Have a follow-up date, or a series of dates, scheduled into your daily activities.
- Anticipation creates intimacy—leave little reminders around the house, like sticky notes with sweet messages.

Kirsten and I have always made it a point to prioritize our relationship. We want the kids to know and see the importance of the bond between their parents. We have never lived near our extended family during our marriage, so we rarely get to call on grandparents to watch the babies. But we hire a babysitter regularly so that we can get out as a couple again. Starting with our very first baby, we made sure to get out of the house, just the two of us.

Your baby's needs are paramount right now, but that doesn't mean your relationship is all about the child for the next eighteen years, because that's not healthy either. That's not a good balance for you or for your children, because it doesn't set a good example of how to maintain a healthy relationship. And one day they will all be gone, and the house will be empty. I adore my children, and I always will, but after about a month or so postpartum, I start to think about when my first date with Kirsten will be. Anticipation builds desire, and with a little planning, I know your date night will be great too.

Sex and Intimacy

If sex during the last trimester was difficult, sex post-pregnancy is even more fraught with difficulties. You and your wife may have low libidos, if any at all—thank fatigue and hormone changes for that. Your wife also needs time for her body to heal, depending on how her delivery went. She may also be experiencing vaginal dryness from low estrogen levels from breast-feeding. She may simply feel uncomfortable with how her body looks, and she will likely experience physical changes over the course of the next year. After giving birth, women's bodies don't magically transform to how they looked nine months earlier. Your wife may still look six months pregnant after she delivers, and it may take a month or more for her uterus to contract to its pre-pregnancy size. Her body needs to release all the various fluids it built up during the pregnancy, which the body removes in the form of urine, sweat, and vaginal secretions. It can take up to a year for a woman's body to return to pre-pregnancy shape, if at all. With all this going on, it's no wonder your wife has little desire for intimacy right away.

However, many men think their sex lives will jump back to the same intensity as before a baby even entered the picture. That's a myth. Your first sexual encounter with your wife may be awkward, painful (for her), or downright unpleasant.

Here are a few ways you can keep your "first time" from being a complete disaster:

- Make sure you're on the same page. Ask your wife how she's feeling. She may look all right, but if she's in pain, sex is probably not on her mind.
- Your wife may want intimacy in other forms. My wife loves when I come up behind her and simply hold her for a moment. Think about ways you can show her that you love and desire her that are not exclusively sexual.
- Physical intimacy is the last thing on some women's minds, especially if they're spending almost twenty-four hours a day nursing or cuddling a newborn. She may be overwhelmed with physical contact. Frustrating as it may be, try to respect that. The baby will grow and become less physically dependent on her.
- Don't jump from no sex to sex. That's a recipe for disaster. You're rebuilding trust, and trust takes time.
- When you do actually have sex, don't expect it to be earth-shattering. Be gentle, kind, and accepting. A dash of humor may go a long way too.
- You may be surprised at how you perceive your wife. Many men struggle with how they view their wives as new mothers, and you may have a hard time looking at your wife as a sexual being again. It's normal and may take time to adjust to your wife's new role.

Bringing a baby into the equation brings psychological changes in men and women—women are generally more in tune with bonding with their children, whereas men may be more interested in bonding with their wives. That's not to say that intimacy can't happen, but remember that your desire for intimacy may be different than your wife's. Though this may cause conflict and stress early on, maintaining an open and honest dialogue will help balance everything out.

Having the Conversation—Talking Points

A common theme throughout this book is establishing open communication, and being able to speak freely with your wife is a crucial part of that goal. How does that conversation go? Well, how you talk can be just as important as what you say. Keep in mind the following points:

- Time your talk. Don't pick a moment when it's total mayhem in the house and you are both just trying to keep your heads above water. Choose a time when the baby is asleep, or perhaps while you're on your date.
- Before sitting down to talk, each of you should make a list of all the ways your spouse makes you feel loved. Once you and your spouse sit down to talk, switch your lists so you can see all the ways you make each other feel loved. Reading these lists can be very powerful. There may be things on the list that you didn't realize make your spouse feel good, and vice versa.
- Think of your tone. Are you nagging your wife about not having sex? Are you saying things like, "You owe me"?
- Discuss contraception. If your wife's menstrual cycle has resumed, she can get pregnant again. Are you ready for baby number two yet? We'll talk more about family planning in chapter 14.

- Keep Colossians 3:19 in your heart: "Husbands, love your wives and do not be harsh with them." We must treat our wives with the highest esteem, as the cherished and precious vessels they are. Speak to your wife with the same respect and honor you desire.

- If you or your wife is angry, it's important to discuss that anger and where it's coming from. Are you frustrated? Is she too exhausted to attend to your needs?

- No one is picking a fight here. Remember that your intention is to reestablish intimacy through communication.

- Consider praying together before talking. Hold hands while you pray. This is a powerful act that will inevitably soothe frayed nerves and permit open dialogue.

Taking one or a few of these steps will help open the channels of communication between you and your wife again. Once you're talking, then you can discuss intimacy. If you still can't have an open conversation, or a fear of intimacy still exists, consider couple's therapy.

Kirsten and I pray a lot individually, but not nearly enough as we should together. Praying together helps keep our relationship strong, but there have been times when we couldn't get back on the same page. We had forgotten that when we met in college, we knew that we wanted to get married and have a family together. We thought of our relationship like a triangle, with the two of us on either side and God at the top. The only way we can grow closer together in our horizontal relationship is when we grow closer to God in our vertical relationship.

After each baby's arrival it can be difficult to remember the bigger picture, that having children in God's image is the endgame. The love you feel for your wife will change—it will evolve from butterflies in your stomach to something more profound and spiritual. Still, we all have these ideas of what a relationship is and how it is supposed to be nothing but bliss all the time. That's just not true. You will encounter difficulties, and you will face situations where you may think you are no longer compatible with your wife. It's so easy to say that a disagreement merits a breakup. Successful marriages are based on working through the tough times. Kirsten and I hit a rocky patch early in our marriage just after Grace was born, and we went to counseling. It helped us sort through the turbulence in our lives, and we needed an impartial third party to help us rediscover the bigger picture.

Postpartum Depression: What You Need to Know

Perhaps you've tried some of the suggestions outlined above to reestablish communication and intimacy with your wife. It can be hard to tell the difference between being crabby due to sleep deprivation and postpartum depression (PPD). It's estimated that one out of every seven new mothers suffers from some form of PPD. Signs of PPD typically appear one to three weeks after birth. While no one knows what exactly causes PPD, scientists have discovered indicators that make some women more likely to suffer from PPD:

- Mother is less than twenty years old
- Family history of depression
- Stressful events in mother's life (difficult childbirth, death or illness in the family, job loss, financial troubles, abusive spouse)

- Pregnancy was unwanted
- Mother has suffered from PPD previously
- Drug and alcohol abuse
- Low thyroid levels

PPD is nobody's fault. It does not make a woman a bad mother, but PPD can be severe.[1] Symptoms include the following:

- Sadness that lasts longer than three to five days
- Feeling panicky and scared all the time
- Feeling inadequacy, shame, or guilt all the time
- Severe mood swings
- Appetite loss
- Loss of interest in enjoyable activities
- Difficulty concentrating
- Difficulty making decisions
- Difficulty bonding with baby
- Recurring thoughts about suicide or killing the baby

If you notice any of these signs, call 911 or your wife's health-care provider. Treatment is available and can help your wife recover.

PPD doesn't just overcome your wife; your child is susceptible to these changes as well. Call your pediatrician if you notice that the baby is crying more than usual, doesn't bond, exhibits behavior problems, or has difficulty speaking later on. Counseling, support groups, and medication can help, and do not be ashamed or afraid to seek assistance if you need it—if your wife suffers from PPD, she is depending on you to make the right call.

You're Talking Again and Ready to Get Intimate. When's the Best Time?

This is the million-dollar question. You're ready to rekindle your physical relationship, but when's the best time? Most likely, the best time is when you and your wife have had a chance to get some sleep. Fatigue is a total mood killer. Try to wait until you're out of zombie mode. Keep working to plan time alone together, and plan couple's vacations when possible. It may take an entire year to get back into the groove, and realistically, your sex life is not going to be exactly what it was before you brought a child into your home. In fact, I think it's even more exciting and unpredictable!

PART 5

OFF-SEASON

CHAPTER THIRTEEN

You Don't Have to Be Perfect to Be a Perfect Dad

In a typical NFL game, everyone goes onto the field with a plan. But situations on-field can change, and players have to be prepared to adapt to various circumstances. The same principle is true with a baby when it comes to raising that child to be a good and responsible adult. Putting a parenting plan in place as soon as you know your wife is pregnant is smart thinking. From there, be ready to adjust and adapt. Without a plan, you're more likely to fumble than you are to score.

What does good parental planning look like? Be prepared to share responsibility. Men continue to take on child-raising roles and participate in family decision making with greater frequency. If you plan on contributing equally to the security and development of your child, you're on the right track for success. Division of labor doesn't have to be fifty-fifty all the time, but the entire family benefits when everyone contributes toward creating a safe and loving home.

How You Can Be an All-Pro Dad

First, remember that there is no such thing as perfection when it comes to being a father. However, the best fathers are willing to learn from their mistakes and make adjustments as necessary. Though plenty of television fathers are portrayed as helpless buffoons, you don't have to stoop to that ridiculous stereotype. Your wife and children do not expect perfection, either. They do expect you to show up, lead, and give them the best of you.

What happens if you're holding down a full-time job? How do you make the time for your family? A father who works outside the home provides the greatest benefit to his family when he comes through the door and picks up the slack. You may be tempted to come home, take off your shoes, and lounge on the sofa for two hours after clocking eight hours at work, but your wife needs you to step up your game. If she's a stay-at-home mother, chances are high that she's ready for a break from the baby by the time you walk through the door. Imagine if you were home with a baby all day rather than shuffling pencils behind a desk, or whatever it is you do at work. You'd be exhausted too.

Remember that being emotionally present is as important as bringing home a paycheck. When Kirsten and I were newly married, a veteran teammate told me about the importance of leaving work at work. He challenged me to make sure that, no matter how great or awful the work day was, when I walked through that garage door I wasn't a football player anymore. I was Kirsten's husband and my kids' daddy. Even if it takes five or ten minutes of sitting in the car and decompressing, the best way to be emotionally present and available is to leave the trials and tribulations of work at work. Your family needs all of you, not just your physical body.

Children also benefit from different parenting styles—that doesn't mean you and your wife aren't working from the same playbook. It just means that you're executing the same play by using different tactics. For example, perhaps your wife uses a softer tone with the children. It's effective, but if you use it, it might not work. While many mothers have a gentle presence, fathers encourage risk taking and are more likely to engage children in challenging activities. Don't baby talk? Don't worry, you're still bonding with your child. Bring your own unique style and influence to parenting. Your baby will be better for it.

Being an active participant in your baby's upbringing should be as important, if not more important, than your career. By stepping up at home, you're demonstrating to your family that child-raising is crucial, and that your presence and participation matter. You're also setting an equitable example for your children by showing that both men and women can share responsibilities around the home.

So, you're sold on the idea of helping out but have no idea where to start? Here are a few simple ways you can be an all-pro dad. Some of these suggestions extend beyond your baby's first year:

- Feed baby
- Change diapers

- Pick outfits
- Dress baby
- Bathe baby
- Wipe tears and kiss boo-boos (more important than it sounds!)
- Blow noses
- Fix toys
- Read stories
- Do bedtime routine
- End fights
- Help with homework
- Assign chores
- Encourage and affirm the members of your household

Your participation around the house shouldn't be limited to interacting with your children. Do your share of bed making, food shopping and preparation, cleaning, dishwashing, and other domestic chores.

Plenty of men who hold down full-time jobs make time to keep their homes neat. For those of you out there who still think domestic chores are strictly women's work, and that stay-at-home mothers don't provide value, think again: Salary.com recently released its sixteenth annual "Mom Salary" breakdown, a survey that estimates what mothers would make if they were paid an annual salary. It determined that stay-at-home mothers who spent forty hours per week with their children would have earned a base salary of $48,509. Factoring in $94,593 from fifty-two hours of overtime, mothers' work in 2016 was valued at $143,102. Mothers working outside the home earned less but still netted an impressive $90,223 in perceived value.[1] So, the next time you think helping out around the house has no value, take into account all the jobs your wife does without pay that keep your family together. She may not bring home a paycheck, but your wife's work has tremendous value. Your participation matters too.

Stay-at-Home Fathers: A New Paradigm

Increasingly, a shift is under way in American households—more fathers are staying home full-time to care for their children, while their wives continue to hold down full-time jobs. In fact, the Pew Research Center estimates that there are over two million stay-at-home fathers in the United States, and that number is likely to increase.[2] This means more men than ever before are shouldering the responsibility of running a household and caring for those in it.

I've met couples who have had difficulty dealing with this scenario because they're concerned that a child raised primarily by a man will not be as emotionally stable as a child raised by a woman. That's a myth. Your baby boy will not grow up to be a "wimp" and your daughter will not be any less feminine. The emotional and mental stability of your children depends on your love and care. If staying at home while your wife works becomes your reality, embrace it. In fact, these may be the most gratifying years of your life.

Fathers and Sons: A Winning Combination

Boys need their fathers. They need to have a strong, positive role model so that they'll know how to interact with people as they mature into adults. Just because a boy is male doesn't mean he'll grow up to be a man—one is determined by biology, the other is taught by example. A father teaches his son the following:

- How to respect women
- Self-confidence
- Strength, sacrifice, and service
- Spiritual leadership
- Integrity
- Unconditional love
- Failure as a teaching tool for success

While you're teaching your son how to be a man, remember that he is an individual and his likes or dislikes may differ from yours. That means if you love sports and your son is more of the cerebral type, don't disapprove of his traits. Nurture them. In addition, don't force your favorite activities on your son.

Imagine the following scenario: You've dreamt of nothing other than tossing the pigskin around with your boy, and finally, when he's around three or four, you take him outside for your first game of catch. You've been building this moment up in your mind for years, and here comes that first throw . . . and it's a dud. You start criticizing your son, saying he should try harder and try again. Your son will try again because he loves you and seeks your approval, but if you push too hard, he will eventually resent these outings. Constant criticism will take all the fun out of activities. He will also feel that he isn't measuring up to what you want him to be. A game of catch should be just that. Keep it light, keep it fun. If he shows talent, cultivate it. If he doesn't, enjoy it anyway. You're creating memories to treasure for a lifetime.

What do you do when you find you have nothing in common with your son? Embrace your son for who he is. Perhaps he'll never make it to the NFL, be a CEO of a Fortune 500 company, or become a doctor. Perhaps your son is a musician or an artist. Love your son for who he is. Guide him; don't try to change him. If your son could care less about Sunday Night Football but loves to paint, break out the brushes and art kit and sit for a portrait. If this sounds frustrating or overwhelming for you, imagine being in your son's shoes, trying to gain your approval and love. If you are willing and open to accepting your son for who he is, you will be successful in maintaining a lifelong bond formed of mutual love and respect.

Daughters Need Their Fathers Too

Daddy's little girl. Three simple words that carry considerable weight. Unlike boys, girls are less likely to mirror the behavior they see demonstrated by their fathers, but girls will seek approval for their actions just as much as any son. A supportive father will encourage his daughter to do these things:

- Strive for success at school, at work, and in love
- Learn self-reliance
- Gain self-confidence and assertiveness
- Seek parity with boys and men at work and at play
- See the value of her inner beauty

Fathers who play catch with their daughters aren't encouraging their daughters to be "manly"; encouraging girls to participate in so-called masculine activities teaches them how to interact with boys and, later on, with men. Additionally, participation in sports teaches girls confidence and gives your daughter a chance to blow off stress. The way you interact with your daughter will directly influence her views on love and friendships. Even when she's a teenager and being rebellious, if you planted the seeds of respect and love, and encouraged open communication throughout childhood, she is more likely to make smarter decisions about relationships.

Studies show that girls who have supportive relationships with their fathers are less likely to engage in risky sexual behavior or get pregnant as a teenager. Girls with strong paternal bonds are also more likely to wait before having sex for the first time, and are less likely to take drugs or drink alcohol to excess.[3] In short, the more quality time you spend with your daughter, the more likely she'll make smart decisions throughout her life. From childhood, you will be the one she looks to for affirmation of her beauty when she puts on her favorite dress. You have the opportunity to set the standard for how she allows every other man to treat her!

How do you put this game plan into action? Here are a few ways you can be a great role model for your daughter:

- Involvement means more than just a quick cuddle or a pat on the head. Play games and read together and, as your baby girl grows, discover what her hobbies are and find activities you can do together.
- Listen to your daughter without judgment. If your daughter can learn to trust you, she will confide in you.

If she comes to you with private questions, keep them confidential—you'll develop respect and trust.

- Be her spiritual leader. Pray with your daughter and share Scripture with her.
- My girls love having daddy-daughter dates. They may happen any time of day, anywhere, as long as it's just me and the girls.

Additionally, the way you treat your wife can profoundly influence how your daughter will think women should be treated. If you want your little girl to reach for the sky, but you tell your wife otherwise, your daughter won't get the message. It's a classic case of practicing what you preach. Always remember that you are your son's first hero and your daughter's first love.

Final Thoughts—Love Is Everything

I've put out a lot of information for you to digest. But I hope that if you remember nothing else from this chapter, you will remember that you are vital in the happy and healthy development of your child. Just as your presence is crucial, so is your method of engagement. When I feel overwhelmed by all this responsibility, I find solace in God's Word, specifically in Paul's celebrated reflections on love:

> Love is patient and kind; love does not envy or boast; it is not arrogant or rude. It does not insist on its own way; it is not irritable or resentful; it does not rejoice at wrongdoing, but rejoices with the truth. Love bears all things, believes all things, hopes all things, endures all things.
>
> 1 Corinthians 13:4–7 ESV

Here Paul is emphasizing that love is paramount, that selfless love feeds everything else in our lives. Love is not only an emotion; it is an action. You will not always feel like being the father and husband that your family needs. It is in these times that true love is exercised because you decide to do what is best for them regardless of how you feel. This is what fatherhood and manhood is all about.

CHAPTER FOURTEEN

Team Expansion

The Second Child and Beyond

Behold, children are a gift of the Lord,
The fruit of the womb is a reward.
Like arrows in the hand of a warrior,
So are the children of one's youth.
How blessed is the man whose quiver is full of them;
They will not be ashamed
When they speak with their enemies in the gate.

Psalm 127:3–5 NASB

Many families start planning for their second child soon after the first has arrived. While your wife might swear that she's never going through the experience of pregnancy and childbirth again, time has a way of erasing the memory of labor and delivery. Kirsten and I knew even before Grace was born that we wanted at least four children. Now we have three girls and two boys. There are advantages and disadvantages to expanding your team, and we'll go through them here. Though I'm biased toward having a larger family, your reality may be quite different from mine. With the right planning, I hope you'll make the best decision for you and your family.

Is there a right time to try for a second child? There's no magic formula, but if you already find yourself wishing that your baby could have a live-in playmate close in age, and you're the type of person who would rather go through potty training and other such developmental milestones all at once, then you're probably ready to have another child.

Advantages Associated with Expanding Your Family

While we come from different sized families, Kirsten and I always knew that we wanted multiple children in our lives. There are plenty of reasons for having more children, including the following:

- The presence of multiple children favors team activities over solitary pursuits.
- Brothers and sisters provide a constant source of moral support throughout their lives.
- Children are less likely to be bored when they're very young if other siblings are around.
- A large family encourages all members to take responsibility for themselves and the people around them.
- Children learn how to share with others by sharing first with siblings.
- Having more children creates more "arrows of change" to shoot into the world.

Of course there are downsides associated with having a large family:

- Parents may have a hard time carving out individual one-on-one time with children.
- Sibling rivalry, gone unchecked, can be disastrous. (Conversely, healthy sibling rivalry can encourage children to reach new heights and test their abilities.)
- Birth order can determine how parents treat each of their children—for example, assuming that the oldest child must do a greater portion of chores than the youngest, even if the age difference isn't great.
- Parents may have difficulty balancing work and home life.
- Children can be expensive.

Larger families aren't as popular in our country as they used to be. According to the Pew Research Center, fertility in the United States has been steadily dropping since the post–World War II baby boom ended around 1964. In 1976, 40 percent of American mothers had given birth to four children. By 2014, roughly the same percentage of women had two children, while only 14 percent of all childbearing mothers had more than four children.[1] Kirsten and I are obviously bucking the current trend in family planning, but we understood exactly what we were getting into and feel our lives are richer for our choices.

Certainly not everyone feels the way we do about large families. Below are advantages to having only one child:

- It's easier for one child to follow the same rhythm as adults.

- The child may be introduced to more cultural outings.
- There are no conflicts or sibling rivalry.
- Overall, most only children have very good self-esteem.
- One child is less expensive.

Many only children earn the reputation of being egotistical and capricious. While that may be true of some, the stereotype does not apply to all. Plenty of children who come from larger families are just as likely to be bratty and overly precocious—much depends on the child's environment. Nevertheless, just as there are advantages to having one child, there are drawbacks:

- Only children may be more easily spoiled and intolerant of others.
- Only children may be more likely to be perfectionists. You may see this as a benefit, and it very well could be, but an unbalanced drive for perfection is harmful to a child's emotional and mental health.
- They may be less adventurous and less likely to take calculated risks.
- Only children may be more likely to miss out on social activities appropriate to their age level, like birthday parties and sleepovers. This is because some parents treat only children like mini-adults and take them to activities adults enjoy, and as a result, they may have difficulty relating to children their own age. (This can be addressed by attentive, supportive parenting.)[2]

Parenting is one of life's greatest challenges. There's no right or wrong decision regarding how many children a family should or should not have. You and your wife need to have an open and honest conversation about how many children you'd like.

What to Do When You Disagree on Expanding the Family

This can be a very difficult situation. In an ideal world, you and your wife discussed how many children you wanted before you got married. Still, feelings and situations change. You're certainly not the first parent to rethink your family plan. Perhaps you have one child, and raising that child has been more difficult than you imagined—you've been dealing with illnesses and extra-long nights awake, and you had to go back to work sooner than you wanted. Maybe your wife suffered from postpartum depression and she's still recovering. All sorts of variables may occur after you have a child that can sway how you feel about having another child. On really bad days, you may question whether having one was too much!

Still, you have to agree on how many children you want. If your wife is bent on having another but you're being held back by ballooning finances, sit down with your financial planner and crunch the numbers. While money isn't the single deciding factor in expanding your family, it is a large component. Seeing where your money goes on paper is a powerful motivator toward better budgeting and fund allocating. You may be able to have baby number two if you are willing to sacrifice some of your material desires—do you really need the six-hundred-dollar iPhone? Are you using that gym membership? If your heart is steering you to yes but your wallet says otherwise, seek outside counsel. You may be able to expand your team after all. And with all that said, plenty of people have large families and don't lead lavish lifestyles. My parents had six of us, and we never missed a meal. God always provided. It is of the utmost importance to seek his guidance when making this type of decision, because his call will not lack his supply. God has a plan for all of us, and if yours includes multiple children, then follow it wholeheartedly. Money is temporary. Family is forever.

When Kirsten and I were still dating, we always talked about wanting children, and how many. As I've said before, we're both detail-oriented people, so we spent hours discussing our ideal family size. Ten years ago, we decided we wanted four children, and after we had four in roughly four and a half years, we started discussing the possibility of having a fifth. I remember thinking, *I'm about done. Or at least, I'm done for now. Let's wait and see.* We waited a few years, and then we ended up having Eden . . . during that period when we were waiting—not trying, but not preventing pregnancy, either! The point is, we did talk about it, and we were on the same page for the first four. Number five came a little earlier than I expected, and I must admit, I didn't handle the news very well. But now, hearing her sweet laugh and looking into her pretty brown eyes, I can't imagine life any other way.

I don't understand how couples get together and don't ever talk about these things, and when the woman becomes pregnant, it's a total surprise. Why wouldn't you talk about that? I think it would be terrible to be married to somebody who wanted four kids and you really wanted two, but you never had that conversation with your wife. Imagine the tension in that household. Such differences could easily break a marriage apart, and I've seen it happen. Fortunately, it's preventable if both parties are willing to have an honest and meaningful conversation with each other. You may not reach a definitive answer right away, but you'll be taking the first steps.

Your Wife Is Already Pregnant Again!

Well, that was quick! Perhaps your wife is already pregnant again—planned or unplanned. When your wife is expecting baby number two (or three or four), providing love and support for her remains as important as it was during the first pregnancy. Don't forget to roll out the red carpet for your wife—rub her back, treat her to a nice warm bath, and plan a special getaway without the baby. Many women feel like their husbands stop being caring and sweet after the first baby arrives. Their husbands think that there's no need for tenderness anymore—they checked those boxes off during the first pregnancy, and now it's back to business as usual. Business as usual these days continues to include providing attention and loving support for your wife. However, being as attentive to your wife during subsequent pregnancies as you were during the first one becomes more challenging—you can't clone yourself and simultaneously provide individual attention to your wife and your baby. I know that after you've read this book, you'll recognize how important it is to carve out time for your wife and child, but you will not be perfect. Don't give up—your family is worth it. You have what it takes!

Pregnancy and Older Children: How to Cope

Perhaps you have children at home already and are wondering how to talk to them about Mom's changing body and the impending arrival of a new sibling. Young children may be afraid that there won't be enough love to go around, or that they'll be ignored when the baby arrives. At Grace's sixth birthday party, Naomi came up to me and asked, "Do you love us more when it's our birthdays?"

What she was really asking me was "It's Grace's birthday right now, and we're celebrating her, so do you love me less?"

I reassured her that, though birthdays are joyous celebrations of life, they don't mean that we love any of our children any less. During subsequent pregnancies, it's important to remind older children that you love them, whether they make you happy or sad or even disobey you. Love is unconditional. Addressing their fears will help them through the process. It's best to discuss their concerns before the baby arrives. Reassure them that their parents love them equally and unconditionally, and that will never change.

Though a new baby may be challenging for your child, the addition of a new sibling can be one of the greatest gifts you give them. That said, sibling rivalry is unavoidable, even when the baby is in utero. To keep tempers from boiling over, here are a few tips that you can use to soothe your child's fears and concerns:

- *Don't keep it a secret.* If your children are more than a year and a half old, they are capable of understanding that a new baby is coming. Of course, you'll have to tailor your explanation to the child's age. Tell them when you tell the rest of your family, and tell them early in the pregnancy. This way they'll have more time to process the news. Children shouldn't hear about the pregnancy from non-family members.

- *If your older child will be moving out of his or her room for the baby, make the move as early as possible.* Moving from a crib or room is a major change. Don't let your child think the move is to make room for the baby. Emphasize that the move is because he or she is becoming a big boy or girl.

- *Bring your children to prenatal appointments so they can hear the baby's heartbeat and see the baby on the ultrasound.* They can also meet the doctor or midwife who will be delivering the baby, and this will make them feel part of the process.

- *Don't expect your children to be overjoyed at the arrival of a new baby, at least not right away.* Try to keep your emotions in check too—younger children may interpret your enthusiasm as transferring your love for them to the newborn.

- *The birth of a newborn should change an older sibling's life as little as possible.* Remind the child of all the things that will be the same—time together, just you two, same toys and books, and same fun activities.

- *Depending on the age of your children, consider where they will be during labor and delivery.* You and your wife may want them present, but remember, there will be blood, and watching one's mother during labor can be very upsetting. Worrying about how your child will deal with witnessing labor is the last thing your wife needs to be thinking about. Consider asking a family member to sit with the children in the waiting room, then invite them in when the baby has arrived.

- *Remember to spend time with your older child.* Even ten minutes one-on-one can make a huge difference in a child's outlook and mood.

- *Do not force your child to love the newborn.* Encourage them to touch or talk to the baby, or even fetch a diaper or blanket. Older siblings should feel welcomed and important, but force will only backfire and may lead to regression and acting out in a misguided way to get attention and affection.

- *Read to your child.* Books can help answer questions your child may have about pregnancy and the new baby. A few books we liked were *We Have a Baby* by Cathryn Falwell and *Welcome, Precious* by Nikki Grimes.

When you're expecting another child, it's important to prepare your children. Depending on how old they are, they might experience joy, curiosity, jealousy, indifference, or a combination of emotions. And no matter how hard you try to maintain an equitable household, there will be sibling rivalry. Again, if you are aware of competition and coax it into positive territory, sibling rivalry can foster a healthy drive for success. Still, we're all human, and it's natural for children to feel hurt about another child entering the family. You can do a lot to keep kids from getting overly upset. Treat every child with respect and remind them that they are important members of the family.

If this whole book hasn't shown you reason enough that fathers are instrumental in the raising of a healthy family, here's another reason: according to research conducted by Dutch scientists, children cope better with the arrival of new siblings when their father is present.[3] No doubt, life at home will get pretty hectic once you return with the baby. If older siblings are under the age of six or seven, consider bringing home a little gift for the older children—not to bribe them, but to remind them that you haven't forgotten about them. Be patient, and they'll come around.

Remember, love is an action, and when you make the decision to love someone, you commit to all the ups and downs that love brings.

Epilogue

Train up a child in the way he should go: even when he is old he will not depart from it.

Proverbs 22:6 ESV

I love my children. I love my wife. They are blessings bestowed on me by the Lord. Sometimes I'm not as thankful as I ought to be. I take their presence for granted. Their questions become irritating; hearing the same knock-knock joke over and over loses its charm. But when I'm traveling for work and I'm alone in a hotel room, there's nothing I wouldn't give to have my loud, noisy, chaotic family right there with me. When I become exhausted by the endless games of peekaboo or being used as a human chariot, I take a deep breath and remember that these moments are precious, and one day these daily activities will fade into cherished memories.

Last off-season, I was reminded of how lucky I am. My whole family was traveling to visit relatives. Since we're such a large group, we've got traveling through airports down to a science—my children are pros at taking off their backpacks and patiently going through security checkpoints. However, this particular trip stood out because nothing seemed to be going right. Our flight was delayed, our seat assignments landed us in separate areas of the plane, and my children were acting like . . . children. Tired, cranky, hungry, excited children. Add the rude stares and "Wow, you've got your hands full!" comments, and Kirsten and I were at the limit of our patience.

Finally, we made it to our seats. As I took a calming breath, I wondered what would be expected of me while scuttling between my children and my wife over the next few hours. Instead of being thankful that we were all on the plane and nothing terrible had happened, I was stressed out. And my kids were still acting like kids—chattering, enthusiastic cherubs, to be sure, but a minute of silence would have been welcomed. As I sat collecting my thoughts, a flight attendant who had been standing in the aisle walked in front of my seat and leaned toward me. *Great,* I thought. *We haven't taken off yet, and already there's trouble.*

"I'm so happy for you," the flight attendant said.

"Excuse me?" I said, caught completely off guard.

"It's wonderful to see such a big, happy family like yours," he said. "I've been married for twenty years, and my wife and I have been unable to have children. You are blessed."

After he walked down the aisle, my heart sank. I felt so sad for this man, and I was embarrassed that I was ungrateful for even a minute that God had entrusted these young lives in my care. It was humbling, and it shouldn't have taken a moment like that to remind me of the blessings bestowed upon me. I think God understands that I'm imperfect, and that little situation was a way to put me back on course.

To say that every day since that flight has been perfect would be misleading. There have been days when I've lost my cool, and others when I've acted so poorly that I've had to ask my children for forgiveness. Overall, Kirsten and I work toward raising our children to respect others, to love one another, and to live in the light of the Lord. We try to teach by example, but we're not always perfect. Our bedtime ritual includes singing one of our favorite verses from the Bible: "Be ye kind, one to another, tenderhearted, forgiving one another even as Christ has forgiven you. Ephesians four thirty-two [*ba-dum, ba-dum*], Ephesians four thirty-two, [*ba-dum, ba-dum*]." I always hope my children sing that song and will internalize those words.

Some days parenting will be a blessing, and other days it will test you. No matter what, we as parents must be willing to teach our children well, to explain right from wrong, and to encourage a life of faith. The best way to teach is to lead by example. Though it is the power of the Holy Spirit that ultimately draws people to himself, all the hymns and Bible verses in the world won't amount to a hill of beans if we don't live what we preach. This means we parents must be willing to admit to our own shortcomings and to ask for forgiveness when we mistreat others, including our children. We're all imperfect, and we're all going to stumble at some point or another. And when we do fumble, we must be willing to ask for forgiveness, even if it's a thirty-five-year-old asking his three-year-old for clemency. Our children may obey us as we obey the Lord and strive to live the life we have been called to, not in our own power, but by that of his Son.

To bring everything back to the gridiron, I once asked a former coach of mine for advice on parenthood. "The days

are long, but the season is short," he replied. I'm grateful
for every one of them and the challenges and beauty they
pose. There will continue to be obstacles on the road ahead,
but I hope to face them with clarity. I am confident that you
will also find the joy and the wonder in raising a happy and
healthy family as well. Your work will not return void. Your
commitment will not be in vain. Always remember, my brothers, you have what it takes to leave a legacy that will bless
generations you may never see!

His descendants will be mighty on earth;
The generation of the upright will be blessed.
Psalm 112:2 NASB

Acknowledgments

I have found that one of the most difficult parts of the writing process is finding someone to believe in your vision. Thank you to the entire Baker Publishing Group family not only for believing in this project but for your desire to empower the millions of men whose families are depending on them to be great husbands and dads. Throughout this journey you have been accommodating in so many ways and I am grateful to be a part of what Baker is doing.

A big thank you to Michael Levin for helping me organize this vision into something communicable and comprehensive. Your contributions made this handbook complete and I could not have done it without you.

Many ideas get lost without the right people advocating for them. Thank you to Ansley Smith and Samantha Baggett of EAG Sports Management and Frank Weimann of Foliolit for being my voice in a new endeavor and representing me through this entire process.

This book is about family. To my mother and father, thank you for showing your six children what it means to love sacrificially, live intentionally, and lead spiritually. Your presence in our lives gave us the foundation to become the adults and parents we are today.

To my five children, Grace, Naomi, Isaiah, Judah, and Eden—I cannot imagine my life without seeing your smiling faces and hearing your joyful voices when I walk through the door. I am so honored to be your daddy. Thank you for your unconditional love.

For years my wife encouraged me to write this book. Time passed and babies were born, yet she persisted because she knew its importance, and she knew the trials I went through as a first-time daddy! Kirsten, thank you for being patient as an uncertain, scared, but excited first-time dad stumbled through our first pregnancy. Thank you for not only birthing the vision for this book but for your insight, commentary, and help in honestly recalling our successes and failures in this adventure called parenthood. I love us.

Finally I thank God for his lovingkindness, faithfulness, and grace. How wonderful it is to call you Father!

Notes

Chapter 2 Pre-practice Warm-Up

1. Jennifer Steinhauer, "Studies Find Big Benefits in Marriage," *New York Times*, April 10, 1995, http://www.nytimes.com/1995/04/10/us/studies-find-big-benefits-in-marriage.html.
2. "Depression During Pregnancy: Signs, Symptoms and Treatment," American Pregnancy Association, 2012, accessed April 10, 2016, http://americanpregnancy.org/pregnancy-health/depression-during-pregnancy/.
3. "Creating Your Birth Plan," American Pregnancy Association, 2012, accessed April 10, 2016, http://americanpregnancy.org/labor-and-birth/birth-plan/.

Chapter 5 X's and O's

1. "Kick Counts," American Pregnancy Association, accessed November 30, 2016, http://americanpregnancy.org/while-pregnant/kick-counts/.

Chapter 8 Make a Budget

1. Diane Harris, "The Cost of Raising a Baby," Parenting.com, accessed November 30, 2016, http://www.parenting.com/article/the-cost-of-raising-a-baby.
2. "Average U.S. Facility Charges for Giving Birth," Transforming Maternity Care, accessed November 30, 2016, http://transform.childbirthconnection.org/resources/datacenter/chargeschart/.

Chapter 9 Scrimmaging

1. "Parents' Guide on Child Safety in and around Cars," National Highway Traffic and Safety Administration, accessed August 4, 2016, http://www.safercar.gov/parents/carseats/Car-Seat-Related-Resources.htm.

Chapter 10 Game Day

1. "Safe Prevention of the Primary Cesarean Delivery," American Congress of Obstetricians and Gynecologists, March 2014, http://www.acog.org/Resources

-And-Publications/Obstetric-Care-Consensus-Series/Safe-Prevention-of-the
-Primary-Cesarean-Delivery.

Chapter 11 Monday Morning Quarterback

1. A. Fleming, C. Corter, J. Stallings, and M. Steiner, "Testosterone and Pro-lactin Are Associated with Emotional Responses to Infant Cries in New Fathers," *Hormones and Behavior* 42, no. 4 (2002): 399–413, accessed June 8, 2016, http://www.ncbi.nlm.nih.gov/pubmed/12488107.

2. Kathleen Berchelmann, "Delaying Baby's First Bath: 8 Reasons Why Doctors Recommend Waiting up to 48 Hours before Bathing a Newborn," Childrens MomDocs, February 1, 2016, http://childrensmd.org/browse-by-age-group/pregnancy-childbirth/delaying-babys-first-bath-8-reasons-why-doctors-recommend-waiting-up-to-48-hours-before-bathing-a-newborn/.

3. "Hugs and Cuddles Have Long-Term Effects," *NIH News in Health*, February 2007, https://newsinhealth.nih.gov/2007/February/docs/01features_01.htm.

4. Benjamin Spock and Robert Needlman, *Dr. Spock's Baby and Child Care*, 8th ed. (New York: Pocket Books, 2004), 51.

Chapter 12 Keeping the Marital Bonds Strong

1. "Postpartum Depression," March of Dimes, March 2016, http://www.marchofdimes.org/pregnancy/postpartum-depression.aspx.

Chapter 13 You Don't Have to Be Perfect to Be a Perfect Dad

1. "Salary.com's 16th Annual Mom Salary Survey," Salary.com, accessed June 13, 2016, http://www.salary.com/mom-paycheck/.

2. Gretchen Livingston, "Growing Number of Dads Home with the Kids," Pew Research Center, June 5, 2014, http://www.pewsocialtrends.org/2014/06/05/growing-number-of-dads-home-with-the-kids/.

3. Linda Nielsen, "How Dads Affect Their Daughters into Adulthood," *Family Studies* (blog), Institute for Family Studies, June 3, 2014, http://family-studies.org/how-dads-affect-their-daughters-into-adulthood/.

Chapter 14 Team Expansion

1. "Parenting in America," Pew Research Center, December 17, 2015, http://www.pewsocialtrends.org/2015/12/17/1-the-american-family-today/.

2. Carl Pickhardt, PhD, "The Adolescent Only Child and Friendship," Psychology Today.com, May 20, 2013, https://www.psychologytoday.com/blog/surviving-your-childs-adolescence/201305/the-adolescent-only-child-and-friendship.

3. M. H. Van Ijzendoorn and S. Van Vliet-Visser, "Een kwalitatieve voostudie naar veranderingen in de relatie tussen eerstegeboren kind en zijn ouders" [The Birth of a Second Child: A Qualitative Pilot Study on the Interactions between Firstborn Child and Its Family], *Pedogogische Studien* 62 (1985): 313–28.

Benjamin Seth Watson plays tight end for the Baltimore Ravens. He attended Northwestern High School in Rock Hill, South Carolina, where he was a football letterman. As a junior, he led his team to the state championship. During his senior year, he caught thirty-one passes for 515 yards and was a two-time All-Region selection and Northwestern High School Student of the Year. Watson was also a member of his school's Fellowship of Christian Athletes.

Watson matriculated at Duke University, where he spent two semesters before transferring to the University of Georgia as a finance major. In three seasons at UGA, he made sixty-five catches for 852 yards and six touchdowns. While attending UGA, Watson met Kirsten Vaughn, a marketing major and collegiate softball player. They married in 2005.

After an all-SEC senior campaign, Watson was a first-round draft pick selected by the New England Patriots in 2004. The Patriots won Super Bowl XXXIX against the Philadelphia Eagles during Watson's rookie year, and the team made it to the championship game again in 2007. In 2010 Watson signed a three-year deal with the Cleveland Browns, where he reunited with former Patriots assistant coach Eric Mangini. He led the team in receptions, receiving yards, and receiving touchdowns that year. Watson signed a three-year contract with the New Orleans Saints in 2013. Named team captain for the 2015–16 season, Watson also had his best season after twelve years in the NFL, earning career bests in receptions (seventy-four) and yards (825), and tying a career high of six touchdowns. In March 2016 he signed a two-year deal with the Baltimore Ravens.

Watson also serves on the executive committee of the NFL Players Association (NFLPA), where he manages and transacts the business and affairs of the association, helps teammates with grievances and fine appeals, and acts as spokesman for the organization on behalf of the teams in surrounding communities.

Off the field, Benjamin stays busy with the One More Foundation, an organization he founded with his wife to carry the hope and love of Christ to one more soul by meeting the needs of those who need it most. He is also an NFL Spokesman for All Pro Dad. In 2015 Watson published his first book, *Under Our Skin: Getting Real about Race. Getting Free from the Fears and Frustrations That Divide Us* (Tyndale Momentum Press).

Benjamin, Kirsten, and their five children currently reside in Baltimore, Maryland.

FOLLOW GOD'S CALL
TO REACH ONE MORE

"Since its inception, One More has been a vehicle to carry the hope and love of Christ to those in our community who need it most, while understanding that the best and most efficient way to reach people's hearts is by first meeting their physical needs."

—BENJAMIN & KIRSTEN

ALL PRO DAD

A program to help you win at fatherhood

"In 2014 I became a national spokesman for All Pro Dad because I realized being a good dad takes more intentional focus and training than being a good football player. All Pro Dad provides practical tips and resources to help you win at being a father. Join me by becoming an All Pro Dad."

–*Benjamin Watson*

BECOME AN ALL PRO DAD

Sign up for the Play of the Day and receive short, daily tips on how to be a better dad.

The Father & Kids Experience is an event held at NFL stadiums. Dads and kids participate in interactive games designed to strengthen their relationships.

Find an All Pro Dad's Day chapter at your child's school. Bond together over breakfast with other dads and their kids.

SUBSCRIBE AT
allprodad.com/subscribe

FIND AN EVENT AT
allprodad.com/events

JOIN A CHAPTER AT
allprodadsday.com

LIKE THIS
BOOK?
Consider sharing it with others!

- Share or mention the book on your social media platforms. Use the hashtag **#TheNewDadsPlaybook**

- Write a book review on your blog or on a retailer site.

- Share this message on Twitter or Facebook: **I loved #TheNewDadsPlaybook by @BenjaminSWatson //** **@ReadBakerBooks**

- Recommend this book for your church, workplace, book club, or class.

- Follow Baker Books on social media and tell us what you like.

  f Facebook.com/ReadBakerBooks

  🐦 @ReadBakerBooks

- Follow Benjamin on social media and tell him what you like about this book.

  f BenjaminWatsonOfficial

  🐦 @BenjaminSWatson